DOUBT BOLDLY

A must read for any struggling Christian doubters. Kenneth Ralph is not a struggling doubter, he's a doubter who is both bold and informed. Neither am I a struggler. If I were, after reading *Doubt Boldly*, I'd be walking with a new spring in my step! We all need others to 'walk with' from time to time, and Kenneth gives us a wide choice. His voice is of a teacher not a preacher; and he reassures that we can walk through the valley of the shadow of doubt without fear of retribution.

Simon Harvey
Educationalist, Musician, Therapist

Hold doubt in your open hand and let it speak. This is the line I will remember from Kenneth Ralph's book *Doubt Boldly*. Doubt is a friend, a guidepost on a journey, a stimulus to personal growth. Don't be fooled, though, this is an iconoclastic look at traditional/fundamentalist religion designed to set us free from its clutches and send us on a renewing personal journey of faith, or *no* faith. Ralph uses personal story, theological acuity and psychological insight to help us on our way. His own journey and experiences are reflected in this work, making it a personal testimony as well as a reassurance for us as we boldly address our own doubts. We are not alone in this.

Charles Gallacher
Minister
Uniting Church in Australia

Kenneth Ralph attentively draws out the effect of radical doubt, particularly in the accessible accounts of people examining their life and faith, some choosing atheism or agnosticism, or progressive forms of faith, others re-confirming their faith. The result is not a book of academic theology, but of engaging storytelling which unearths vivid details showing how individuals, famous or leading everyday lives, have tackled the big questions of a human life: how to understand its meaning; how to live; how to make a fair society; how to face mortality. *Doubt Boldly* is an ambitious undertaking, exploring its themes with nuance and thoughtfulness.

Hermina Burns
Poet and podcaster
author of *Barbara Tucker: The Art of Being* (MUP)

Kenneth Ralph sympathetically addresses readers who have religious doubts about Christian doctrine and teaching. He provides accessible suggestions and examples of how to examine religious doubts, with a detailed step-by-step process for those who like a structured approach. The writings of significant scholars and their challenges to orthodox views about Jesus are explored with sensitivity. This is particularly helpful to those who want to examine which parts of the Christian message these scholars have accepted or rejected and their reasons for doing so. Some readers may find this section challenging as it may be the first time they have come across traditional core beliefs about Jesus being revised or dismissed in this manner. Readers are encouraged to undertaking the challenge, with the knowledge that it can have positive outcomes and may lead to an invigorated faith.

Dr Ruth Webber
Honorary Research Fellow
Catholic Theological College, University of Divinity.

FAITH & UNCERTAINTY IN
CONTEMPORARY CHRISTIANITY

DOUBT BOLDLY

KENNETH F. RALPH

COVENTRY
PRESS

Published in Australia by
Coventry Press
33 Scoresby Road
Bayswater VIC 3153

ISBN 9781922589538

Copyright © Kenneth F. Ralph 2024

All rights reserved. Other than for the purposes and subject to the conditions prescribed under the *Copyright Act*, no part of this publication may be reproduced, stored in a retrieval system, or transmitted in any form or by any means, electronic, mechanical, photocopying, recording or otherwise, without the prior permission of the publisher.

Scripture quotations are taken from the *New English Bible*, copyright © Cambridge University Press and Oxford University Press 1961, 1970. All rights reserved.

Catalogue-in-Publication entry is available from the National Library of Australia
http://catalogue.nla.gov.au

Cover design by Ian James – www.jgd.com.au
Text design by Coventry Press
Set in EB Garamond

Printed in Australia

Doubters are explorers.
Anson Cameron

*... the mature religious sentiment is ordinarily fashioned
in the workshop of doubt...*
Gordon Allport

*If you would be a real seeker after truth, it is necessary that
at least once in your life you doubt, as far as possible, all things.*
René Descartes

*It is both senseless and impossible to expect modern minds
to accept mythical, pre-scientific views of the world
as part and parcel of Christian teaching.*
Rudolph Bultmann

*I am a Jew, but I am enthralled by the luminous figure
of the Nazarene ... No one can read the Gospels
without feeling the actual presence of Jesus.*
Albert Einstein

The Galilean has been too great for our small hearts.
H. G. Wells

Also by Kenneth F. Ralph ...

'Anger Management and Interpersonal Skills in the Community' in *Teacher Wellness*, Deakin University 1993

'At the Bedside' in *Willing to Listen and Wanting to Die*, Penguin: Collingwood 1994

Yes, I get Depressed, Joint Board of Christian Education: Collingwood 1996

Your Final Choice, Morning Star Publications, Melbourne 2015

Contents

Foreword ix

Part 1 The case for doubting boldly **1**

1   Welcome to a Religious Doubters Festival   3
2   Eight bold doubters   7
3   'I have de-Christianised myself'   19
4   Late onset religious doubt   29
5   Has Christianity ever had to do a major U-turn?   44
6   Managing the doubt process   65
7   Heresies, ancient and modern   75

Part 2 The revitalisation of Jesus studies **93**

8   The challenge to orthodox views about Jesus   95
9   Putting new clothes on Jesus
    Albert Schweitzer's search for the historical Jesus   106
10 The onion man of biblical interpretation
    Rudolph Bultmann and de-mythologising   113
11 Jesus as Subversive Sage
    The Jesus Movement of Robert Funk and others   123
12 Jesus according to the feminists
    An alternative to patriarchal religion   134

Part 3   Real people, real dilemmas   **151**

Brace Bateman
Thank you, Christianity   152

John Coulson
So, What of Jesus?   154

Simon Harvey
Embracing my doubt, finding my freedom   157

Sigrid Jacob
My religious/spiritual journey   160

Anne McClelland
Becoming myself   163

Amanda Swaney
My view on religion   166

Afterword   168

Endnotes   171

Foreword

Religious doubt is best seen as a friend, not an enemy. It is a legitimate act of self-affirmation. It helps us find new answers to new questions. It opens doors to surprises, fresh ideas and liberation. It helps keep our spirituality alive and adaptive. Done with boldness, doubt has a lot going for it.

Bold doubt is also known as radical doubt. It involves digging deeply into the roots of belief, examining them, keeping what is deemed sound and discarding what no longer works. Martin Luther, the robust Father of Protestantism, encouraged believers to *sin boldly* but also to *believe more boldly in Christ*. To that religious narrative comes my invitation to *doubt boldly*.

For some, doubt appears as an autumn leaf falling gently to the ground. Others put up a stiff fight against their doubt as soon as it makes an appearance. Then there are those who keep their doubts in the mists of their awareness before finding the courage to let them say what they want to say.

Not all will need or want to go down the doubt path. When I asked a good clergy friend whether he ever felt a need to take a second look at his Christian beliefs and values, he replied, 'Never. I have always had a policy of delighting in what I do believe in and not giving much attention to what I don't believe in.'

Bold doubting will lead some out of religion, which is how it was for medical journalist Michael Mosley, author of the international best seller *Fast Diet*. Doubt can also lead to a reinvigorated faith, as in the case Charles Birch, Professor of Biology at the University of Sydney (1961-1984), who replaced religious fundamentalism with something far more enriching. Each of their stories is discussed in chapter 2.

Generally speaking, those who feel the strongest need to reject or re-do their faith are likely to be those whose religious upbringing featured the following: a strong dose of moral 'shoulds'; Christianity presented as the one true way; scepticism about modern science; a low regard for the human condition; a highly elevated view about the authority of Christianity's sacred book and a divine requirement for a blood sacrifice.

Occasionally, the opposite is true. Some are on the search for a religion with more authority and vigour. They characterise what they are abandoning as easy-going liberalism which is strong on love, but soft on responsibility and moral duty.

Doubt is best seen as a friendly sibling, always on the lookout for fresh or alternative explanations for how things work and for choosing which guides to follow when exploring the challenges and contradictions of being a person. Of course, doubt can be carried too far, as in nihilism, the belief that there are no enduring values or foundations on which to build the good life. Doubt can also be grossly underdone, as in the closed mind that Jesus referred to in his famous agricultural image of the farmer spreading seed that falls on rocky ground. Neurotic doubt — an obsessional mind activity which gives little rest or satisfaction to its owner — is also possible.

Radical doubt in Australia these days is found mostly in Baby Boomer territory, those born between 1946-1965. There is a simple explanation for this. Gen X (born 1966-1980) initiated the goodbye to Christianity, and those that followed them – the Millennials, Gen Z and Gen Alpha – are not much into it because so few of them ever had it the first place.

This book is not written to promote Christianity or, for that matter, any other religion. Nor does it support the unsupportable, that if you have a religion, then Christianity is the best pick, but failing that, any religion is better than no religion. In my view, there is a cluster of secular authors who are more than adequate in helping us find our way along the smooth and rough tracks of life. Peter Singer and A. C. Grayling are two examples, and many are finding the ancient Stoics a helpful guide on how to live the good life.[1]

I write from the perspective of Christianity. But surely it is safe to assume that various levels of doubt are commonplace among the adherents of all religions.

I gained immeasurably from becoming a Christian in my late teens. I also think I am a better person for having jettisoned a great deal of what mattered so much to me back there. My selfhood and my way of engaging with my outer world have been enriched by a regular pruning of my faith tree, allowing new growth.

The book falls into three parts. Part One looks at the doubt process from various perspectives. Why doubt is inevitable and therefore normal; how to manage it; the role doubt plays in building a heathy-minded religion; the various pathways and outcomes to which scepticism leads us. Part One also highlights the big trouble in which some find themselves if certain self-appointed minders of orthodox Christianity find out what they are doing, or, as they see it, going too far in so doing.

Part Two focuses on the re-vitalisation of Jesus studies in recent times, for a good reason. Many who are troubled by institutional Christianity are not so by the Nazarene.[2] This section contains a cluster of brief profiles of Jesus as presented by biblical scholars and how they answered the question posed by him in the Gospels: 'Who do you say that I am?' (Matthew 16:15). There is precious little agreement among them, which is no big surprise, since Jesus himself was not much given to saying who he was, as that section illustrates.

Part Three contains the responses of six good friends who responded to my invitation to write an 800 word 'something' about religion as they have experienced it. What a treasure chest of personal statements about how religion makes its impact on us! Indeed, something can be said for reading this section first. It contains great stories on the various changes that some have made to their religious faith. My book is *about* doubt. Their stories are about *living with* doubt.

Part 1

The case for doubting boldly

Chapter 1

Welcome to a Religious Doubters Festival

In which are described several sub-types of letting go of former things

Imagine a Religious Doubters Festival. See it as a rich display of diversity about how to be a doubter. Some in the full flush of jettisoning what no longer works for them. Different degrees of angst. Different outcomes. Different time frames for doing what they are doing. And different language to encapsulate the experience.

Some at that festival would simply be content to describe themselves as old-fashioned doubters, none-too-fussed about giving up some of what they once believed in. Others would tell a tale of a complete crossing over to the other side, and feeling better because of it. Some might want help to get the job done in a hurry. Some will be content to be one of Aesop's turtles.

Some at this festival would describe themselves as de-Christianising. They have shed or are shedding various beliefs or practices they once deemed indispensable. The Oxford Dictionary definition of 'de-Christianise' rings bells for them: 'to deprive or divest of (its) Christian character'.

This chapter describes eight various sub-types of these de-Christianisers, or as this book calls them: bold doubters.[3]

FULL DE-CHRISTIANISERS have given away the whole thing. Folk who do this have decided no longer to give themselves the name Christian. Once it was an identity statement. Not anymore. The beliefs, rituals, ethics and practices of Christianity fail to evoke any resonance in their hearts or minds. It's as though they have gone back to the tattoo parlour and erased an image which once portrayed who they were. Chapter 3 is about a full-time clergyman who gave Christianity away with the words 'I have de-Christianised myself'.

Full de-Christianising does not imply that the individual has replaced Christianity with something else such as a full-on switch to agnosticism or Confucianism or Islam or Hinduism or a bristly Dawkins type atheism. It *may* be any of these, but not necessarily so.

PARTIAL DE-CHRISTIANISERS are those who are engaged in the spring-cleaning of their faith house. They are working out what to keep, what to modify, what to throw out. What they aren't doing is abandoning the premises, as is the full-on de-Christianiser. This spring-cleaning involves them in divesting themselves of the specific beliefs, values or practices of Christianity. For example, they may say that they have de-Christianised Sunday. By this they mean they have said goodbye to strict Sunday observance, which was once a key part of their Christian commitment. They have now given themselves permission to peel the potatoes, chop wood, clean shoes and have a game of tennis on Sunday, all of which previously were out of bounds. And, if once they were very strict Presbyterians who attended the quarterly Saturday night pre-communion service, they would now not be obliged to follow the clerical recommendation that they keep themselves from physical intimacy that night, before the following Sunday morning's Sacrament of Holy Communion.

Multitudes of beliefs and practices can be questioned, changed, discarded: truth telling, the marriage contract, God as a miraculous interventionist, the resurrection of Jesus, the Ten Commandments, abortion, attitudes to other faith, military conflict and so it goes on and on.

In short, everything on the Christian agenda is open to re-evaluation. Some are inclined to rank beliefs into an order of seriousness. For example, low order items include whether it is permitted for a Christian woman to use lipstick and wear above-the-knee dresses, or whether God gets very upset on hearing rude words. Moderate order items might refer to issues such as whether lying can ever be a good thing, whether wars can ever be just, why Paul was uninterested in the historical Jesus, and how far forgiveness should go. High order items could include the divinity of Jesus, LGBTQI, the trustworthiness of the Bible, the Trinity, the killing of self or others, whether the bones of Jesus still lie in Palestinian soil.

SOMETHING-IN-THE-MIST DE-CHRISTIANISERS. These are those who sense something occupying the mists of their awareness, asking to be scrutinised. Perhaps this something has been sitting there for some time, unnamed and unowned, intriguing some, alarming others.

RESISTANT DE-CHRISTIANISERS are those who can't or won't admit to themselves that the doubt bell is ringing. No spring cleaning for them. They bat away any deviation from the past. To open themselves to their doubts would upset the foundations on which they have built their lives. Far better, they tell themselves, usually unconsciously, to affirm the opposite and if that doesn't work do more of it until it does work. Insistent affirmations about what they do believe can be their antidote to admitting and examining uncertainty. Going along with the crowd also protects them from the fear of being the only one in their community who doesn't believe in this or that.

HOSTILE DE-CHRISTIANISERS. The *de* words these folks prefer are *detoxing, decontaminating* and *delousing. Decapitating* is up there too when punitive anger is at work: angry at their parents and/or the church for propagating so much religious nonsense; angry at themselves for being seduced by such nonsense; and angry for investing so much energy which now seems misspent. Some ruminate on this rage for a long time and become its victim.

SILENT DE-CHRISTIANISERS. These are those who consciously keep silent about their doubts or faith reconstructions. Perhaps they feel no need to go public about this new faith position. In other cases, they correctly foresee that the cost of going public will be more than they are prepared to pay. As author Mick Herron has one of his characters say: *there are some beliefs you're supposed to keep under wraps if you don't want to be excommunicated.*

RELIEVED DE-CHRISTIANISERS. These are those who, while not popping their champagne bottles, exhilarated by their spiritual spring-cleaning, feel a sense of liberation. Getting rid of this or that has opened the door to new freedoms and perspectives. In his magnificent *Pilgrim's Progress*, John Bunyan's character Christian felt that a great burden was lifted when he became a Christian. Some Christians feel the same relief at jettisoning Christian beliefs that no longer have the ring of truth or which bind their behaviours with too many restraints.

SMUG DE-CHRISTIANISERS. These not only feel a great deal of satisfaction about having given away some or all of their previous beliefs, but also possess some on-going need to blow their trumpet about what they have done: a self-congratulatory see-how-smart-I-am sound off.

There we are. Eight different groups all gathered for one weekend event, under one conference tent, to share various stories about the ebbs and flows of religious sentiment. Maybe that melancholic Melbourne poet Leunig could get the show going with a reading of his poem:

> *As I was learning how to live*
> *I came upon the narrative,*
> *Well wait a minute, let me see,*
> *The narrative was dumped on me*
>
> *So in good faith I stayed with it,*
> *Although it didn't seem to fit.*
>
> *But time goes by and things go wrong*
> *And then the soul must move along*
> *As many narratives commence*
> *To not add up and not make sense.*
>
> *What crazy power-hungry ghost*
> *Decides for all what matters most?*[4]

Chapter 2

Eight bold doubters

Individual Christians change their minds about a vast range of ethical and doctrinal issues. This chapter describes some of them. You might even see yourself reflected in the stories.

Clover: *The Sydney Mayor in trouble with her church*

74-year-old Clover Moore, Sydney's longest serving Lord Mayor, is a good example of someone coming to conclusions about what she believed and not only finding them to contrast with the orthodox beliefs of her Church but getting into trouble for going public on the subject.

The first popularly elected woman (2004) in the job, she was brought up a Catholic. But she had, as she put it, 'to separate (her) beliefs from the failings of the institutional church'. She believed that being a person of a faith was part of her 'personal strength'. Now (2023) in her fourth term, she says the tougher her mayoral job has become, the more she has prayed. But the institutional church – put out by her departure from traditional teachings – has been 'very unhappy' with her, especially on the issue of her public support of the Sydney Mardi Gras and same-sex adoption legislation. She notes that when a complaint was made to a local priest about her, he asked her what she had been doing to upset the Church. She replied that in her understanding, attendance at Mardi Gras on Saturday night, followed by reading the lesson in Church the next day had not gone down well.

She sees Christ as a 'real radical', citing the example of him taking on the establishment by throwing the money changers out of the Temple. When asked if she is now *persona non grata* at her local church, she says that this is certainly not true of the people engaged in what she sees as the real work of the Church on the ground. She also observes that it is possible to 'shop around to go to Mass.'

Clover finds her way in these pages because she typifies those public persons who, while dissociating from the specifics of mainline religious teaching, have reconstructed a faith that works for them.[5]

Sophie: *the not-very-churchy Christian*

Sophie's (not her real name) disillusionment, on the other hand, would lead her far away from organised religion. She says, 'I am not very churchy these days. I used to be. It was part of growing up with my dad, who was a regular lay preacher. But he was full of criticism about others. At our meal times, we grew tired of his narky views'.

She asks: 'Doesn't the Bible say "Judge not that ye be not judged?" But here he was, always judging everyone'. She describes how her slow disillusionment with her dad seeped into her own religious commitment.

She gave away going to church. But some things stayed with her. The deep spirituality of the Psalms was one. She liked the way in which they understood the ups and downs of human moods. Generally no lover of Paul, she was nonetheless attracted to his question, 'If God is on your side who can be against you?' This helped her find a way through her problems. She typed the statement up and stuck it on her fridge door.

She hasn't given away the regular reading of her prayer book. She doesn't know if these prayers do much to change things for others, but when she does go to her quiet spot each night, she feels a deep calm. She says she may not be a full Christian, but various parts of her remain responsive. Once in a while, she goes to Sunday worship, but less and less. She suspects she will give up organised Christianity altogether one day.

Johan: *the secular Christian*

If Sophie is a God believer who gave up on the church, Johan (not his real name) is the opposite. He is a non-believer who regularly attends Sunday morning church. If Sophie has done a de-Christianisation on the formal church, he has done one on its deity. He says, 'I am not very religious these days, but I have kept the Christian morality'. He no longer believes in prayer. During worship, he tunes in and out of the things his minister regularly emphasises: divine grace; forgiveness of sins; the beauty of the Bible; celebrating the Christian year; soul nourishment through the sacraments; the parables of Jesus and so on. These big ideas did get his full attention in his undergraduate days, but not any longer.

What keeps him coming to worship on Sunday? 'My wife', he says with a smile, 'but it is really my church's social ideals that I am committed to. My church's public support for fairer income redistribution, refugees and climate issues: that's what keeps me here'.

Some might say his unbelief in God disqualifies him from calling himself a Christian. He says others can see him that way if they want to, but he has no trouble believing in a secular kind of Christianity, one that is very low on ideas about God but high on community service.

Rejecting his earlier Christian beliefs has resulted in his giving away the doctrine part of his church's religion – especially the salvation and spiritual growth bits – but not its social ethics. He is open to being persuaded that there could be a God, but not the God of his primary school years. He says, however, that he would be a hard nut to crack on this issue. He is content with his religion the way it is. He is also of the view that a lot of his mates are like him. He said he Googled the phrase *secular Christian* and was pleased with what he found. He thinks he may be part of future!

Michael Mosley: *Science wins over religion*

Michael Mosley (1957-2024), science journalist, medical school graduate, author of the best-selling book *The Fast Diet* (plus many more on this subject) and well-known TV presenter — he of the genial smile and erudition on all things medical — is a classic example of someone whose doubt led him to science as a better way. There is little in the public arena about his personal life, but the Saturday morning *Age* did reveal a few details of his view on religion. His maternal grandfather was a Church of England bishop in Hong Kong, and several others on the maternal side were missionaries.

He says he lost his own faith, or at the least started to question, during his studies at Oxford University. His father, who was never a strong believer, handled this OK, but he thinks his mother still hopes he will 'come back to the Church'. His sister is still a believer, but neither of his two brothers remains committed. He does have a faith, he declares, but it is science-orientated, particularly in the current COVID crisis. He writes of 'the power of science to respond to crises'.[6]

Pamela: *the name and claim doubter*

This near on fifty-year-old, women was once a full-on Pentecostal believer. But not anymore. The 'name and claim' idea is what brought her down. Strange that, because it was once what brought her in. At the centre of her Pentecostal faith was a loving, miracle-working God who offered her a full, victorious life, surrendered to Jesus after full immersion baptism. Filled with the Holy Spirit. Gripped by the conviction about God's power to perform marvellous things.

'Name it. Claim it.' Her pastor regularly preached. By this he meant that Christians should be bold in asking God for specific miracles. She decided she would. She would ask God miraculously to heal a breast cancer which had returned after six years in remission. Her oncologist made recommendations about appropriate treatment. Pamela shook her head and said 'No! This time God will fix it. All things are possible to him'. The oncologist knew her patient well enough not to dispute this conviction.

Eight weeks later, as arranged, she was back. Tests showed the tumour gone. Pamela called it her first miracle. She had named it, claimed it, and got it. All glory and power to God. Her specialist said 'Yes. It was a miracle. You are very fortunate'. The doctor also had another name for such an occurrence: spontaneous remission of symptoms. It was a phenomenon well documented in medical journals. She also told Pamela she had come across it twice in her practice. Pamela smiled, nodded her head, but said nothing in response. Her name for it was God. That was enough.

Bit by bit, on the strength of this one victory, she named and claimed other issues close to her heart. That her husband would become a believer. That her grandson's temper tantrums would subside. She also joined with fellow women believers at Tuesday morning prayer meetings during which they shared God's marvellous interventions on their behalf. Not always, and not even often, but enough to reinforce their beliefs. They didn't see God's intervention as magic. They didn't think they were entitled to what they wanted. What they saw was a compassionate, miracle-working God coming now and then to their aid for their good and for God's glory.

Then bad winds blew in. Pamela developed a severe skin infection that kept her awake at night, making her grumpy and critical. Her pastor's marriage came undone, an awful shock to the congregation. Her husband's indifference to God turned into hostility. Her grandson's tantrums began to take the form of violence towards his mother. She followed her church's protocols for examining what inner sins and faults might have accounted for her fall from divine grace, but nothing brought inner peace or resolution of her troubles.

Her Name and Claim belief began to unravel. Readying herself for Sunday morning church, once a full-on pleasure, was now tainted with irritation, confusion and, worst of all, a nagging doubt. Within six months, she was seriously on the way out. The early stages of her anger focused on God, the church, and her plausible, guru-style pastor. Then it turned inwards to herself. How naïve she was, she told herself, about the whole business. She gave herself a tough time on this issue. But that anger was also to pass.

She now knows what she doesn't believe. She is not too sure about what she does believe. But she does know she hasn't crossed into atheism. She feels she is rebuilding something more realistic. It seems to be working for her. 'I call myself a Christian', she says, 'but I am not sure where it is all leading'.

Charles Birch: *From Fundamentalism to Panentheism*[7]

Now to the case of an Australian bold doubter, geneticist Charles Birch (1918-2009) who for 23 years was the Professor of Biology at the University of Sydney. Birch was brought up as a low church Anglican in Melbourne. Promoted there was 'Sin, saving souls, a literal interpretation of the Bible, miracles and the efficacy of the sacrament of communion', all 'parts of a total package of Fundamentalism'.[8] He arrived at adolescence with a picture of himself as not good enough and very sinful. And he entered university studies at Melbourne University with what he called a compartmentalised brain: one part science and the other religion. But things changed when he did graduate studies at the University of Adelaide. His colleagues there were either atheist or agnostic and his supervisor, Dr H. G Andrewartha (with whom he was later to co-publish a book *The Distribution and Abundance of Animals*) thought it strange that he took religion so seriously. Andrewartha's view was that religion was 'anti-science and the source of much evil in society'. As a result of conversations with Andrewartha, especially when they went into desert country on field trips, Birch felt quite unable intellectually to defend his position. He came to see that his religion was 'full of holes'.

What he didn't know at that time was that Charles Darwin had experienced the same dilemmas. Darwin also believed in the literal truth of the Bible. On his famous voyage in the Beagle, Darwin amused the officers with his naive orthodoxy and was highly shocked when one of his fellow officers declared his disbelief in the Bible's account of the flood. Birch muses that had he known that he and Darwin had each experienced the same dilemma — attempting to reconcile religion and science — he would have been encouraged.

But there the parallel ends. In Darwin's case, the scientific theory resulting from that voyage led to the death of his religion. For Birch, meeting a science that was hostile to his religion during post graduate studies stimulated a radical reinterpretation of his faith which harmonised his religion and his science. He credits the Student Christian Movement at the University of Adelaide for showing him an alternative. Somewhat surprisingly to him, some of the elements of what he called his first conversion in his fundamentalist days came back to him. They were (i) a renewed experience of forgiveness, (ii) the courage to face the new, (iii) a sense of not being alone in the universe, and (iv) the values of life as revealed in the life of Jesus.

But this second conversion created a new problem which was to occupy him, he writes, for the rest of his life. He was dissatisfied that science presented him with what he described as 'a mechanistic universe which provided no clues to the meaning of life's fundamental experiences of value'. Science also had 'nothing to say about feelings', what he later called the *subjective side* of nature. He writes 'I started a new journey of discovery'. He found Panentheism — the religious philosophy of Alfred North Whitehead — that proposed that 'God is in the world or nowhere, creating continually in us and around us'. For Panentheists, God is not a divine being separate from all other beings. God is integral to all that exists, intimately connected to all life processes. This view of God appealed to Birch, who was discontented with what he called the *mechanistic view* of universe which, in his view, prevailed in science. Birch sees no conflict between science and religion, affirming that we are absolutely dependent upon the scientific approach. Without it, he wrote, we would be lost 'just as we were lost before science got into the picture'.

In 1990, Birch was awarded the 1990 Templeton Prize for progress in religion, and wrote several books on the interrelation between science and religion.[9]

Phillip: *A big-time doubter about the Creed*

A few years before his death, a good Victorian mate of mine, a low church Anglican, said he estimated he had risen to his feet in church about 2,500 times to say the Apostles' Creed, Christianity's favourite. But at the time of his telling me this, he believed in only five of the roughly 25 items of the Creed. They were:

1. I believe in God.
2. I believe in Jesus.
3. I believe he was crucified.
4. I believe in the Holy Catholic Church
5. I believe in the forgiveness of sins

The other twenty items which once he believed, he no longer accepted as true: God as Father, God as Almighty, Heaven, Hell, the virginal conception of Jesus, his descent into hell after his crucifixion, his resurrection and ascension, the life everlasting, and so on.

Phillip's disbelief in these doctrines did not happen overnight: he thought perhaps over a decade or longer. In his early doubting phase, he said he voiced all the words each Sunday along with his fellow worshippers, but was practising silent mental dissent. Then gradually he said out loud only the ones he continued to believe in.

Eventually, he decided to come out about this non-belief to his Vicar, just to set the record right. He said he got the response he expected. The Vicar made no big deal about his declaration. Phillip surmised the Vicar also had his doubts, but didn't enquire in that direction. What Phillip was prepared for did not come to pass. He wasn't moved out of the leadership position which he occupied in that congregation. And he continued to read the books of John Shelby Spong, USA Episcopal Bishop who, he said, did not initiate his doubts, but did help him work through them.

Phillip – the thinking-man Christian – did not raise with the Vicar some specific questions: if Jesus went back to heaven to re-join the Trinity, from which, according to the creeds of Christendom, he had originated, did he still carry his humanity with him? If so, how much of a problem was that to the workings of that divine Threesome? He thought that it was best not to provoke the Vicar too far.

David and Mary: *A Catholic couple in crisis over contraception*

David Lodge is a self-described child of a lower-middle class London family, son of a devoutly Catholic mother. Born in 1935, he was to become Professor of English Literature at the University of Birmingham and one of England's most recognised novelists. His engaging autobiography[10] is in large part a tale of his disengagement from traditional Roman Catholicism to what he describes as a more progressive position.

He and his wife Mary had each been brought up as conventional Roman Catholics. That meant no sex prior to marriage, no artificial contraception and a recognition that the primary purpose of sex was procreation. As he wrote: 'Our belief that artificial contraception was a mortal sin was as firm as our belief in the divinity of Christ or the doctrine of transubstantiation – indeed firmer, since it was easier to grasp'.[11]

By the time they married, he at 24 and she 25, the issue of contraception had to be faced and resolved. Off they went off to a Catholic Marriage Advisory Council where Mary received information about 'how to chart' her monthly cycle in order to use the only form of birth control sanctioned by the church: The Rhythm Method, also known as the Safe Method.

'We blithely placed our faith in it', David recorded, but within three months of their wedding Mary was pregnant. This was not planned. They were ill-prepared. And for the first – but not the last – time, child bearing resulted in Mary's having to postpone her progress in her desired career path. Eager not to have a second child quickly and before they 'resumed sexual relations', as he put it, they paid another visit to the Catholic Marriage Advisory Council. There they were instructed in *perfecting the safe period of woman's monthly cycle by use of a rectal thermometer*. He sardonically observes that this lasted for about a year. And since Mary did not take up the advice proffered by their landlady's mother that she *just pull away dear... pull away at the last moment*, Mary again fell pregnant. A second child arrived, a boy. And then a third, also a boy, born in the early hours in their bedroom. They named him Christopher.

By early afternoon, he had been diagnosed as Down Syndrome, or as their doctor of that time called him, a Mongol. They were advised to place him quickly in a mental sub-abnormal hospital, but when the staff refused to show them around the wards, they decided against that course of action. After the initial 'profound shock', they were determined to give Christopher as normal a life as was possible without a detrimental effect on his brother and sister nor on their own relationship.

In one respect, David notes, the arrival of Christopher led to 'a positive improvement in our marriage'. Advised, as they were, that mothers who gave birth to Down Syndrome babies were more likely to have another and given that it was going to be demanding enough bringing up one, they made the decision: Mary would go on the Pill.

Lodge notes that this decision was enormously powerful. It signified that they were taking responsibility for their own lives. They were 'not being governed by a code invented by theologians, one which looked increasingly irrational and had no demonstrable basis in the teachings of Jesus Christ.'[12] He also observed that going on to the pill 'led to the great enhancement of our intimate life'.

By now the early 1960s, David and Mary were describing themselves as *progressive Catholics*. He went public in support of moves within Catholicism to overturn the ban on artificial contraception. Then, in 1969, Pope Paul VI reiterated the traditional ban in his encyclical *Humanae Vitae*. Lodge joined with 100 academics from ten countries protesting the decision and pleading for a more flexible response on the issue. No longer would he endorse Catholic teaching. He went public with his view that 'the church teaching has undoubtedly had tragic consequences for countless lives, in sexual deprivation, marital stress and damage to women's health'.[13]

Subsequently, both he and Mary joined the Catholic Renewal Movement, a lay association that agitated for a regeneration in the Church. The concluding comment in his biography *Quite a Good Time to be Born* is that in researching and writing another work, *How Far Can You Go?* (winner of Whitbread Book of the Year 1980), his faith had been demythologised. He writes, 'I had to recognise that I no longer believed literally in the affirmations of the Creed which I recited at Mass every Sunday, although they did not lose all meaning and value for me'.[14]

Worth noting

Several observations emerge from these examples of folk who put some or all of their religion under review.

- Most did this re-working of their faith while still in association with their church. Their doubts did not lead to waving a complete goodbye either to God or organised religion or both.
- Upheavals in religious sentiments can be initiated by disturbances in relationships or selfhood.

- Commonly, a discarded religious view is replaced with an alternative one, which makes it a re-Christianising rather than a de-Christianising.
- Although the doubt process can be painful, destabilising and stressful, most claim to have moved on to a better personal place as a result.
- Disillusionment about clergy behaviour can trigger or reinforce doubt.
- Resolving religious doubt does not happen overnight nor in a fortnight. Sometimes it takes five hundred fortnights.
- Dislodging one piece of the belief system is liable to cause instability in some of the surrounding beliefs.
- Religious doubt is seldom a one-off event. It commonly becomes a lifelong process.
- The impact of a significant other person can be decisive in faith formation and change.

What none of these cases illustrates is another possibility. Faith changes can occur without our knowledge or consent. We simply come to a surprising awareness that somehow, somewhere, something has shifted within. And this discovery is greeted with approval.

Chapter 3

'I have de-Christianised myself'

The case of a famous modern clergyman who gave it all away

Joseph Fletcher couldn't do much about it, but it was commonplace for him to be introduced in worldwide public meetings as the 'infamous Red Churchman'. Sometimes, this was intended as a putdown. Other times, he noted, it was 'humorous and accepting, but still a bit skittish'. We are not sure which of these it was when in 1950 an Australian Bishop introduced him this way, on the occasion when he and another 'Red Dean' barnstormed Australia on a national how-to-make-peace program.

An ordained USA Episcopal clergyman, Fletcher was certainly no stranger to fame and controversy. He arrived in Australia with a track record of high-profile involvement in USA social justice causes which included opening up labour unions and solidarity with Black Americans. More than once he was arrested or imprisoned for this advocacy. Twice he was violently attacked – on one occasion by five men with their fists, on another beaten unconscious with tyre chains in a dark spot in the woods.

Little wonder that he attracted the attention of the 1940-50s Joseph McCarthy witch-hunt against communists. He was one of the first clergymen required to appear before what was officially known as the House Special Committee on Un-American activities, a notoriety he seemed happy to accept, even celebrate.

Fletcher's fame had grown for more reasons than his social justice activism. He wrote numerous articles and books on ethical matters from a Christian point of view. In *Situation Ethics*, his most famous book, he married the secular utilitarianism of John Stuart

Mill and the *agape* love ethic of Jesus of Nazareth. Published in 1966, the book was translated into several languages and proved to be his most controversial written work. Deemed the father of biomedical ethics – he said he invented the word *bioethics* – he is credited with writing much of the early ideological underpinning for the international Right to Die movement.

Then, in 1967, at the age of sixty-five, after forty years as an activist clergyman and academic, he retired from the Christian ministry. Nothing unusual about that: most clergy are more than ready to step away by their mid-sixties. What astounded one and all was his announcement that he had, as he called it, de-Christianised himself. By this he meant that he had voluntarily given up his belief in all Christian ideology. He was no longer a Christian. He now described himself as a humanist, no longer a theist. His memoir[15] describes in detail the reasons for this. He repudiated the lot, becoming a 100% de-Christianiser. He was able to do what so many clergymen like him cannot: declare openly his slide into atheism or serious agnosticism.

Fletcher had no church experience prior to theological training and ordination. His mother was 'wholly non-church,' and his father a lapsed Catholic. But his association with an Episcopal rector inspired in him the hope that he might be able to restore that which Christianity had 'buried and lost sight of': its 'tremendous imperative for social justice'. He notes that had he been asked why he was entering the Christian ministry at the time of candidature he would have replied 'because I want to do good in the world'. Social ideals led him to Christianity, he declared, not Christianity to his social ideals. As he put it, 'my focus was passionately on Christian social thought and action, not Christianity as such'.

After ordination, he had served as a pastor in the United Kingdom (St Peter's, London) and in the United States of America (St Paul's in Cincinnati). He also taught Christian Ethics and Labour History at Episcopal Divinity School, Cambridge, Massachusetts and at Harvard Divinity School. He gave speeches world-wide and wrote numerous articles and books on Christian ethics.

But in time, without his recognising it, something, he claims, was 'eating away' at both his pro-Marxist and Christian ideology. He referred to this as his 'pragmatism' or his 'non-creedal bent', certainly something incompatible with any grand ideology.[16] Mainstream Christianity's opposition to medico-ethical issues such as abortion, voluntary euthanasia, termination of badly defective newborns, voluntary sterilisation and divorce also greatly disturbed him.

But whatever it was that was eating away underground had not yet surfaced. He was fully committed to developing a new Christian ethic which, despite his de-Christianisation, is still listed among the various types of ethics deemed Christian. He situated this new ethic between what he called two other types of Christian ethics: legalism and antinomianism.

Legalism enters each situation which requires a moral decision underpinned by a set of rules and regulations leading to *directives* to be followed. The Old Testament Ten Commandments of Moses provide us with a perfect example.

Antinomianism assumes that you approach each new decision-making situation with zero principles or rules. You are 100% against them, hence the word antinomian: anti=against and nomos=law. Fletcher notes that St Paul had to confront two strands of this approach to moral decision-making. One claimed that the Risen Jesus had freed them from law. The other argued that they would intuitively know what to do if they listened to what the living spirit of Jesus was saying to them.

Fletcher called his new approach *situation ethics* or *consequentialism*. Later in life, he called it *case ethics*. His critics labelled it the New Morality, a term intended to be dismissive. Situation ethics puts people at the centre of concern and attempts to calculate what is best for them. Their welfare will depend on the facts of each new situation. There may be a Yes to terminating a badly defective newborn at birth in some situations, but not in others. Truth-telling might be the best result in one situation, but harmful in another. Suicide can be rational and moral in one circumstance, but not in another.

Central to Fletcher's avowedly Christian ethic is the moral maxim of Jesus as stated in the Gospels: 'you shall love the Lord your God ... and your neighbour as yourself.' (Luke 10:37) He dubbed this an *agape* ethic. He writes: 'Only one "thing" is intrinsically good; namely; love: nothing else at all'.[17] Not love as liking or desiring or emoting, but as a disposition, an attitude to the other. In his view, both Paul and Jesus 'replaced the precepts of the Torah with the living principle of *agape* – good will at work in partnership with reason. *agape* seeks the neighbour's best interest'.[18] *agape* is not sentimental love, nor liking, nor reciprocal; you don't get anything back. *agape* is non-congenial outreach for the deserving and the undeserving alike.

Fletcher also found support for this ethic in Paul's Letter to the Philippians 1:9: 'And this I pray, that your love may abound yet more and more in knowledge and in all judgment'. He claims to find here the four pillars of the Christian ethic method:

1. a prayerful reliance on God's grace
2. the law of love, presented as the norm
3. knowledge of the all the facts in the particular situation
4. judgment, which he calls decision making; 'a matter of responsibility in humility'.[19]

Fletcher had various ways of describing this *agape* ethic: 'thoughtful love, careful as well as care-full';[20] 'goodwill at work in partnership with reason'[21] and consequentialism.

In August 1982, Fletcher was scheduled to speak at the Fourth International Conference of *Right to Die Societies* in Melbourne. Illness caused him to withdraw. The paper he had planned to present, read in his absence, claimed that case ethics compared with rule ethics chooses whatever course 'seems the most desirable one in terms of human wellbeing'.

Five steps are necessary in reaching such a judgment:

1. specify all the foreseeable consequences
2. predict the consequences of each of these possibilities
3. estimate the probability of these consequences
4. appraise the desirability or acceptability of each of these consequences
5. decide which alternative appears to hold the most beneficial results.[22]

This process of making a moral judgment by assessing the benefit or otherwise for individuals and society will appeal to some but not to others. But if you have to decide whether to bring a fertilised egg to full term, or whether grandad was right to shorten the distressing and painful end of his life by Voluntary Assisted Dying, then this way of working out the right and the wrong could appeal.

This case ethics approach certainly found acceptance in the bio-ethical world where hard decisions were called for daily, and explains Fletcher's regular appearance as a speaker at various International *Right to Die* seminars promoting voluntary euthanasia legalisation, and participating in symposia debating abortion, rational suicide, infanticide, in vitro-fertilisation, income redistribution, divorce, embryo-splitting and the sexualising of relationships.

Fletcher indicated that this situationally-oriented ethic was applauded in the fields of medicine, public administration and social work, but was generally condemned by the orthodox among Christians, Jews and Muslims. Marxist journals also joined in the attack. Those who are critical of situation ethics claimed it to be a gross perversion of the notion of love, too demanding, too variable in outcome, and wholly unacceptable because of its repudiation of the Moses ethic of ten moral absolutes binding for all persons in all ages for all situations.[23]

Even so, opposition to his views from within Christianity does not seem to have contributed to his moving into atheism. Fletcher clearly enjoyed the jousting with colleagues, adversaries and audiences on the subject of his new ethic. Moreover, he was receiving sufficient positive feedback from many of his generation. What also helped, he claimed, was that he did not seem to be a person of great hatreds or angers. Tolerance, he once wrote, can stretch a long way if hate can be kept out.

If he did not depart from Christianity on account of hostility, nor stay within it because of the goodwill and excitement of some, what did explain that exit? Part, he claims, had to do with his discontent with formal Christianity's poor track record on social and personal ethics. Comparing the medico-ethical and social justice approach of the two Geneva-based organisations with which he was familiar – the religious World Council of Churches and the secular WHO (World Health Organisation) – he found himself more often in sympathy with the non-religious one. Christian social ethics, he maintained were 'not giving any significant help'.

There are legitimate questions to be asked about his claim. After all, fellow clergyman Martin Luther King was writing, speaking and marching in the cause of social justice at the same time that Fletcher was being harassed by segregationists. There was also the famous Walter Rauschenbusch, Social Gospel theologian and New York Baptist pastor, who taught at Rochester Theological Seminary. His was an ethical Jesus, not a saviour from sin Jesus. Child labour, fair wages, tax reform were his concerns. Fletcher, of course, was aware of him, but expressed his view that although he (Rauschenbusch), and a few others like him, were 'ethically perceptive,' their work 'lacked adequate theological sophistication'.[24] Fletcher would perhaps concede that although theirs were strong individual Christian voices, they were not the voice of corporate Christianity.

If Fletcher found both the social and personal ethics of Christianity lacking, he was equally or even more critical of its dogmatic side, which gets a colourful lashing. He decided, as he put it, to take a 'hard look' at the Christian doctrine itself. By this he meant 'the whole repository,' of 'God, Jesus, revelation, sin, salvation'.[25] He examined Christian doctrine on 'its own merits' as he put it.

When Fletcher set himself to this task, he concluded that 'the whole thing was weird and untenable',[26] indeed that the classical foundation of Christianity was 'an absurd story' about a God who creates the world, permits people to be as wicked and weak as they choose for a long time: 2000 years in fact. This God then picks out an 'obscure peasant in Palestine to redeem the world', decrees that the only way a human being can avoid eternal damnation, which he places in front of them, is by believing that this Palestinian peasant is 'by divine power their only way of escaping his condemnation and eternal suffering'. He is their Saviour. He 'fixes everything up just right for the believers. But "not" for his fellow creatures if they don't believe'.

In basketball terminology, this is one big slam-dunk on doctrinal Christianity, occupying just eight lines in his *Memoir*. It is a vivid, radio grab caricature of what in theology is called the penal substitutionary theory of the atonement. Moreover, he makes no mention of various other narratives of the Jesus story presented by historic Christianity. Nevertheless, many in Christianity will nod approvingly at his take down of this blood sacrifice motif so popular in the hymnody, prayer books and Sunday sermons of certain branches of Christendom. One last thought about the slam dunk. Perhaps Fletcher was doing what many do when departing something: embellish or distort the explanation in order to make it seem more plausible both to themselves and to others.

What is clear is that, despite Fletcher's dump, it does not appear that he behaved as a grumpy, antagonistic de-Christianiser at the time of his departure. In 1967, he indicated to the students at the Episcopal Theological School that he would no longer be able to officiate or take part in chapel services. As an 'alienated or unbelieving theologian', as he put it, he could not, in good faith, continue to provide those services. There is no record of how they received it, nor the response of his fellow theological college clergy, nor the officialdom of the Episcopal Church in America, the communion to which he belonged as a clergyman.

What the record does show is that when Fletcher did depart the church, he did so, he writes, 'with lots of thanks to it for so many things'. For forty years, he reported, he had lived in the church, so there was some 'ambivalent sense of loss.' But he also noted that leaving was an experience of 'freedom and comfort, of mental calm. 'No dark night of the soul', just the opposite. He also noted that he 'left it to keep faith with myself'.[27] I take that to mean that whatever got him into Christianity in the first place (i) could no longer sustain him personally and (ii) failed to tick the boxes reasonably required of ordained clergy. He walked. He wasn't pushed. He had outgrown it. He no longer saw himself as a Christian. Why present himself as one?

One novel twist is that he left with a view of himself as 'still a theologian'.[28] He explained this by indicating that he meant that he had a 'special knowledge of theology.' Presumably, most within the church would have expected that he would have given up that name for himself. The concept of a fully de-Christianised theologian sounds a contradiction in terms – or to use a flavour of the month word – oxymoronic to them. Obviously, it didn't to him.

What did surprise Fletcher about his renunciation of Christianity was that, at his 'ripe old age', as he put it, a 'totally new career' opened up for him. No one, he wrote, would believe how much more he would learn, and how much he would accomplish therein. He would, he wrote, be medicalised and biologised. He accepted the invitation to take up a new appointment as the first Professor of Medical Ethics in the School of Medicine at the University of Virginia, the beginning of a career that was to span fifteen more years (1967-83).

If up to 1967 he had written half a dozen books, sixteen chapters for symposia, twenty-one pamphlets and fifty-four articles, by 1984 he had more than doubled that amount. He lectured, wrote learned articles, made speeches world-wide, and authored four significant books on bio-ethical matters. He received the 1981

Beecher Award in Medical Ethics and was made a laureate of the Academy of Humanism.

At the very least, Fletcher's story illustrates (i) that once a Christian does not mean always a Christian; (ii) that the end of something can also be the start of something else and (iii) that not all faith transitions are turbulent, stressful or problematic. Fletcher was at pains to emphasise that he ought not be viewed as a 'harassed or embattled person'. At no point did he ever feel that way, perhaps, as he wrote, because he always had 'plenty of ego strength'. People who hated or challenged his ideas always, he asserted, seemed to like him personally, as he did them. He put this down to his natural liking for people and an easy way of relating to them. Moreover, because he was not a 'sorehead type or loaded with hostility', he was not kept out of things. Quite the contrary, he saw his life as being full of comradeship and acceptance.

Fletcher liked to use the word *radical* about himself. For him this word was not a synonym for 'extreme'. Properly it means, he wrote, 'going to the roots' of a question or a problem.[29] He is the epitome of a bold doubter.

I salute him and if I were in the business of dedicating a book to someone, which I am not, he would be a good candidate for the front page of this one. Clearly, I have a soft spot for him. For several years in the mid-1970s-mid 80s, I ran local seminars in church settings about his New Ethic and was amazed at the positive reception. Independent thinkers, or those looking for something different, found his ethic a breath of fresh air especially on issues of abortion, voluntary euthanasia, sexual ethics, IVF, homosexuality, truth telling and rational suicide. It gave them an approach to working out for themselves what makes something right and something wrong from a Christian viewpoint.

In the 1980, I corresponded with Fletcher. I invited him to lead a series of seminars in outer Melbourne sponsored by the church of which I was the minister. In a warm reply letter, he expressed regret at having to decline. His health had deteriorated and he was cutting back on overseas commitments. It looked as if he had personally typed his letter on one of those old-fashioned Olivetti manual typewriters we all used in those days. I surmised the famous man no longer had a secretary to do his correspondence. I regret that he was unable to accept my invitation. He seems to me to have been what Australians call 'a really good bloke.' He was to die a few years later, in 1991. He was 86 years old.

Chapter 4

Late onset religious doubt

Harvard university psychologist Gordon Allport proposes that faith formation progresses through three stages.[30] First is *raw credulity*, most clearly evident in children. They believe in what they see and imagine, and what they are told. Most transit out of this phase. Some don't. They stay with the religion of their childhood. Allport describes their faith as *childish, authoritarian and irrational*.

The second stage is *disruption*. Doubts emerge, commonly in late adolescence and young adulthood. Allport labels this *teenage mutiny* and claims that this phase is *an integral part of all intelligent thinking*.

The third and last stage is *mature belief*. It painfully grows out of the to and fro of *alternating doubts* and *productive thinking*.

A key question is: if most individuals transit out of their childhood religion in late adolescence or young adulthood and often in a rebellious mode, is religious doubt best done at that stage of life; if, it is postponed, will it be accompanied by the same sort of rebellious spirit? The short answer is that laying down a challenge to one's religion can be done at any time and does not necessarily emerge as a defiant breakout. Late onset doubt may lack teenage exuberance and defiance, but this is more than made up for by the relief and the rewards the process brings. Admittedly, there are not many these days in Australia who are doing an Allport faith transition and most of them will not celebrate their 60th birthday again, but it is never too late to make faith changes.

So first a few words about teenage mutiny then a switch to its gentler form in the late years.

Teenage religious mutiny

As Allport claims, faith changes are commonly associated with puberty, powered by the pursuit of self-determination. Bold doubt is at work here, perhaps crossing into full-fledged mutiny. Many inherited values and beliefs take a hammering at this teenage life stage. There is no reason why inherited religious views should be exempt from this scrutiny. At this stage if life, ideas about God can be subjected to a big working over. Attitudes to the Bible undergo a challenge. Miracles seem baloney. Grace at meals can be passively/aggressively undermined. Calisthenics or cricket becomes more appealing than Sunday sermons and old-fashioned hymn singing. Praying for world peace – or anything for that matter – seems stupid or infantile. Rules-based religious ethics, with their emphasis on obedience to external authorities, have little appeal.

As inevitable as this teen mutiny might be, the current crop of Australian teenagers is not into it. There is a simple reason for this: you can't mutiny against something you never had. Nearly every grandparent reading this sentence will understand this. It was their offspring who gave the goodbye wave to the beliefs and practices of Christianity. And what is for sure is that they didn't indoctrinate their children in religious concepts. The grandchildren of the current group of grandparents have no need to rebel.

We can say with confidence that most teenagers of this third decade of the third millennium are very likely to have never been inside a church, except for Grandma's funeral or the occasional wedding, nor read a Bible nor heard a sermon, nor prayed, nor felt any need to thank any god in any universe for anything. We have now arrived at a position at which, according to a 2016 survey, the largest current group of young Australians are 'nones'. That is to say, they do not identify with a religion or a religious group. These Gen Zs have little or nothing to do with organised religion in their personal lives, although a significant proportion are interested in different ways of being 'spiritual'.

The authors of this survey claim that the current group of teenagers fall into six types in their attitude to religion.

1. *This worldly* (23%) In their own words, they have no space for religious, spiritual or even non-material possibilities. They are non-believers in God and do not see themselves as humanists or secularists. As one respondent put it they are 'science-y'.
2. *Indifferent* 15% This group is undecided about it all.
3. *Spiritual but not religious* 18% They sit between 'this worldly' and 'seekers' (below) but God plays no part.
4. *Seekers* 8% Seekers describe themselves in this way but consult horoscopes, see a psychic or both.
5. *Nominally religious* 28% They identify with a religion, but faith is not important to them. They are culturally committed to follow the religious identity of their parents, but do not darken the door of a temple, church or mosque.
6. *Religious committed* 17% Religion is a big part of their lives. They are mainly Christian (Pentecostal or Evangelical) or Muslim. They attend worship and believe in an afterlife.[31]

Late onset religious doubt

If most of today's youngies are therefore not into red hot religious mutiny or settled disbelief and their parents are very likely to have completed the task, who then is? Traces of it can of course still be found in all generations, but amongst one group it is readily observable. Hello to grandma and granddad, the current group of Baby Boomers. Among them we now find a cohort subject to late onset, serious doubt and debate. As in the case of their children and grandchildren, some are abandoning ship, or have long since done so, perhaps crossing into agnosticism or atheism. Others, like the Gen Zs above, are either trying out a spiritual path which does not involve them in organised religion.

There are, however, some who are reluctant to quit. They are likely to be the main readers of this book. They continue to support their local church, and are often the backbone of vigorous social justice and human care programs associated with their congregation. They mow the church lawns, look after the finances, visit shut-ins, play the organ, sing in the choir and serve on the plenitude of committees that keep the institution going.

Some of them see themselves as the last tenants. *For Sale* notices take their attention on the front lawn of other local churches and they reluctantly admit the day may not be far off when one will be erected outside their own beloved building. They read the data and it is not good. Take the Uniting Church in Australia. In June 2023, its quarterly magazine informed them that in 1961, 20 per cent of Australians were either Methodist, Congregational or Presbyterian; by 2021 the same was true of only 4%. Moreover, the rate of decline for the Uniting Church was one of fastest among the denominations: down 37% in the years 2011 to 2021.

Regardless of what some foresee as the terminal decline of organised Christianity in Australia, our cohort of faithful Baby Boomers refuses to bail out. They tell themselves that God is alive and well. They see their task as keeping their hands to the plough, doing the work of the Kingdom in their own way in their own patch. It is among this group that we find some for whom societal and personal life changes are triggering faith changes. They are the late-onset bold doubters. The senior years of life are presenting issues for which their previous Christian values and beliefs seem no longer appropriate. Divorce, sex and death are just three issues for which fresh approaches are being sought by these late-onset doubters. In question form they are asking:

- Are divorce and remarriage a no-go zone?
- If I re-partner, but not marry, is it OK to sexualise that relationship?
- Can I call myself a Christian if I don't believe in an afterlife and now believe in Medically Assisted Death?

(i) *Late life divorce*. Another way to put that question is this: if my marriage is not working, even though I have tried everything to fix it, am I obliged to stay in it? The data indicates that the rate of divorce in senior years in Australia is rising, despite the overall rate slowing down. But a religious road block against uncoupling, a moral *No No*, can be hard wired into the conscience of some believers. Their early Christian belief that marriage is designed by God as a permanent partnership, refuses to die. In the past, they even took the obligatory marital vow which included 'Till death do us part'. And very likely, the presiding minister quoted the words attributed to Jesus: 'What God has joined together, let no one separate' (Mark 10:9) sometimes translated, 'let no one put asunder'.

Marital separation is seldom undertaken lightly, and is nearly always a high-stress process. Linking it therefore with a don't-do-it from God can be a double whammy for some, locking them into an ever-worsening state of marital distress. Others make the move and uncouple from their partner, but fail to silence the voice of religious censure. An accusing conscience continues to haunt them and in various ways can create disturbances in any new relationship.

Then there are those who do the double uncoupling. They leave behind both the dysfunctional marriage and the censuring ethic. They challenge the teachings of their church that claim that the Bible is solidly against divorce. They do some reading of contemporary biblical scholars and are perhaps surprised to learn that the Jesus words of prohibition on divorce (Matthew 5:31-32) are not so black and white as they appear, or indeed may not even have been uttered by him at all.

They come to the view that the Old Testament and Roman codes about how to regularise our intimate and social relationships may have been appropriate for those times but not ours. In short, these bold doubters have done a constructive re-educating of a badly educated conscience. And if that clause about not undoing what God put together worries them, they may find solace in the views of some modern Christian ethicists who say that maybe God didn't do the uniting in the first place. Certainly, all Christian consequentialist ethics will stress the greater damage done in some marriages by staying, rather than by leaving.

(ii) Senior Sex. Put differently, the question on this issue arises: do I have to say no to some of life's pleasures now that my relationship status has changed, now that I am going solo? What these late onset doubters chiefly have in mind is sex. Their 'mutiny' is against the traditional Christian ethic that sex is legitimate only for those in a marriage and only between a man and a woman, and in some quarters, only when the purpose of it is the making of a baby. All neatly summed up in the traditional notion of pre-marital chastity and marital fidelity.

The reason these seniors are raising doubts about this old religious code is that the loss of their partner by death or divorce has resulted in the forming of a new relationship in which sex is beginning to surface. Most of these Baby Boomer individuals are not pursuing casual or recreational sex. They are thinking of relationship sex between two people involved in an ongoing, non-marital, commitment. This relationship might lead to marriage, but not yet and perhaps not ever. Neither party is selling their own house. Joint ongoing occupancy of one house may or may not be involved. There is no amalgamation of finances.

A common scenario is that one of them is open to sexualising the relationship but the other is saying No. She – it seems more commonly the woman – is held back by her old Christian ethic of sex only in marriage. Other issues may be in the mix, but the big one is about not going against her religiously-informed conscience. The desire part of her says Yes. The conscience part says No. She is aware that her children had sexualised more than one relationship before settling into one, steady, live-together partnership. The same, she knows, was also the case with most of her friend's offspring. Indeed, in some of these cases one of their grandchildren acted as pageboy or flower girl at the ceremony when the relationship was subsequently legalised. Given that little or no harm has come of any of this, at least in those cases, why, she is asking herself, should non-marital sex be outlawed in religious ethics?

Fortunately – although some say disastrously – some sections of official Christendom are listening and seem prepared to move away from their long-held position on sex. To my surprise, my own Uniting Church in Australia has even floated this possibility.

Its 1997 General Assembly Task Group on Sexuality[32] addressed the question of how to decide whether or not to engage in sexual activity. The Task group document presents what is called an 'ethic of character'. This is different to an 'ethic of rules', which they assert is bound to fail, because, they claim, humans have a 'natural resistance to commands'. Character ethics, they propose, focuses on the kind of people Christians want to be and are called to be as Christ followers who reflect the grace and faithfulness of God.

This ethic of character, the committee indicated, focuses on a cluster of key questions to answer when deciding to sexualise relationships. Will it enrich or enhance relationships? Is it consensual, fully respecting another's No? Will it create harm or cause long term distrust? Does it reflect a faithful, committed relationship? What impact might it have on the wider community of faith? What about the opening up of possible vulnerabilities in either?

I doubt this Task Group material surfaced much in the pulpits of UCA congregations. Historically, there has been too much push back from Sunday worshippers when sexual issues have been discussed in the worship service. But it was used in some local Christian education programs in which subjects such as sexuality are deemed entirely appropriate for discussion. Individual clergy also reported their use of the key questions in group pre-marriage programs and pre-wedding interviews with couples.

(iii) *Death and Dying*. Our third issue concerns the inevitable arrival of the Dark Horseman of Death on our piece of turf. The nearer he approaches, certain issues take a livelier hold on our attention, two in particular. One: is this all there is? Two: if my dying is really nasty and painful, can I bring it to a quicker conclusion? Unsurprisingly, the answers we find in our faith box – decades old in some cases – may not appeal to us anymore. A reworking is called for.

In our earlier years, we may have feared dying. Now, as it comes closer, we note that this fear has abated or disappeared altogether. Angst about the *fact* of death is replaced by worries about the *how* of it. The alarms bells are now more likely to ring about cancers, respiratory issues, cardiac faults, diabetes, kidney dysfunctions, and the various symptoms and types of cognitive decay.

What some now fear in the senior stage of life is that the last weeks, months, or even years, will be severely compromised, demeaning, and, worst still, involve unrelievable pain. As theologian James Gustafson put it, sometimes the powers that bear down on us can be stronger than the powers that sustain us. Some have nursed a loved one through months of a nasty end-of-life process. They are dubious about the claim, made in certain medical quarters, that unrelievable terminal pain is a thing of the past. Nor do they accept the proposition of certain branches of religion that suffering tests and refines faith, provides a context for trusting in God's providential care, opens up the possibility of courage in the face of adversity and rewards the faithful with benefits in the world that lies beyond this one.

Little wonder then that some slowly find their way to supporting proposals for the individual's legal and moral right to actively hasten death. Once it was for them that God and/or nature determined the boundaries of life and death. Now their narrative is that there can be circumstances in which they can accelerate their dying. What they were formerly opposed to – Advanced Care Directives and Medically Assisted Dying – are now ethically welcome. They may have even lodged the appropriate forms in the right place.

Whereas in former years they may have thought that the gods of the universe, including their special One, made these ending of life decisions, now they think otherwise. Hans Kung, a one-time darling of the Roman Catholic Church, but subsequently banned from the ranks as an official teacher of theology, was raised on the belief that death is something God gives or ordains. But accompanying his brother through a twelve-month period of a terrible dying was the trigger for a complete reversal. God, he claimed, not only gave humans life and with it the invitation to live responsibly and generously, but also 'the utter right to self-determination', which, he wrote, is not withdrawn at 'the last phase of our lives'.[33] He became one of Christianity's most famous advocates for voluntary euthanasia.

Late stage heightened awareness of mortality also triggers questions about what comes next. The closer death gets, the less sure some can be about what they once believed. It is the immediacy of the thing that arouses their need to take a fresh look at traditional beliefs about death. Jacqui Tafell, *Sydney Morning Herald* journalist and editor, wrote that when cancer 'stormed in from left field', as she put it, giving her mother an all too brief remaining life, she, Sue, gave a strict instruction to Jacqui: 'When I go, tell people I *died*' (my emphasis). Sue wrote about how much that helped. When people offered condolences for her loss, she winced and felt that her mother would have too. She wasn't lost. She wasn't passed on. She hadn't gone to a better place. 'We know exactly where she is', wrote Jacqui, 'Under the camellia bush at the house she and Dad built and shared more than sixty of their seventy years together'. It was the same when her parents' ashes were scattered. Sue continued: 'So please, on her behalf, no euphemisms or platitudes. No resting, no passing, no losing. No shuffling off this mortal coil, joining the bleedin' choir invisible. Her name was Sue Taffel, and she is dead'.[34]

Whether Jacqui or her mother did at one time believe in the more after death, but moved away from that belief, is unclear. What is clear is that an increasing number of modern Christians have made that journey. They are big time doubters about the afterlife as usually presented to the pew sitters of Christianity. The new storyline for some of them goes like this. No personality survival after brain death. No consciousness. No eternal soul idea. No future life. No angels or deity waiting to greet them at the Pearly Gates. No marvellously transformed body. No grand reunion with loved ones who preceded them in death. No trumpet sound welcoming them to eternal bliss with their friendly God. 'Dust to dust, ashes to ashes' is all they want said at their funeral. Absolutely

'No' to the words so regularly used by the clergy: 'in sure and certain hope of the resurrection of the body to everlasting life'.

They subscribe to what is sometimes called the full stop (.) theory. Everything that constitutes the person ends in brain death. The only way they survive is in the memory bank of others or as particles in the soil or ocean. There is no *more*. They are not saying there is no God or that their God belief is not strong any more. For them God is continuous. Humans aren't.

Other Christians do believe in human continuity but different from that described in the Bible or presented by mainline Christianity. They hold a semi-colon (;) view of death. Reincarnation for example, or re-absorption of their spirit in a divine World Spirit from which everything emerges and eventually returns.

Then there are those who can't make up their mind about what happens after death. A question mark (?) symbolises them. They have decided to live with uncertainty. Their agnostic view is that there is possibly *something* rather than *nothing*, but it is also possible there is nothing rather than something. These folks are not necessarily God deniers. Nor are they are taking an each way bet. Some are traditional Christian believers, except on a few specific issues including this one. They can also have a high view of the Bible and Jesus and some still say their evening prayers.

Making funeral arrangements can be a bit of a problem for bold doubters who have moved away from the traditional Christian view that there is more after death. Some have even been known to say to a well-liked parish clergy person: 'When you officiate at my funeral, which I hope you will, please don't talk about the bliss of heaven and the hope of the resurrection. I don't believe in them anymore'. They are not renouncing Christianity, just one of its traditional beliefs. They are still God believers. But their God is for and in the now. The delights, the tasks, the rewards, are also in the now. They neither seek nor expect more than this.

Even so, there is something audacious about asking an ordained clergy person to conduct a funeral service which lacks themes about heaven, resurrection, eternal peace and the delight of reunions. The odds of compliance are not good. Most clergy will decline, and reasonably so, on the grounds that if you don't want a Christian funeral don't come seeking such a ceremony from me.

Sex. Divorce. Death. These have been our three discussion points. They illustrate that life's circumstances can be triggers for faith and value changes in the later years. Inherited religious values can reach a use-by date or be inappropriate for all of life's changing circumstances. Alternatives can be sought and found.

Healthy-minded v Neurotic religion

Late onset doubt emerges in some as a suspicion that their religion has been more sick than healthy. Not all of it and not all the time, but still likely to falling short as a steady source of help in making sense of existence, creating constructive bondings with others and working out how to do some good somewhere on the big issues of the planet. And some would say that is putting it far too mildly. My religion, they claim, was bad for their mental health, buggered up their relationships and didn't deliver on its promises.

There are many variations on this theme. And the specialists in this field, some hostile, some friendly, have a variety of opinions. Many uncomplimentary words have been used about religion: pathological, neurotic, dysfunctional, infantile, magical, malignant, outdated, primitive, an opiate and so on. It is not hard to find heaps of evidence to support these claims. An alternative view is that religion has a Janus face – two contrasting, conflicting aspects – capable of great good and capable of great harm.

Senior citizen believers certainly possess a good viewpoint from which to look back on their experience of religion and chart the highs, the lows, the nasties and the virtues of their religious story. Bitter sweet some will say. And some will be open to the possibility that in degrees or substance their religion was more sick than healthy. American philosopher and psychologist William James, brother of Henry the novelist, made this contrast between sick and heathy in the Gifford Lectures on Natural Religion at Edinburgh in 1901-1902, published under the title *The Varieties of Religious Experience*.³⁵

Healthy-minded religion, he argued, minimises the presence of evil in the world and makes much of its goodness. He wrote that persons in possession of a healthy-minded religion 'passionately fling themselves upon their sense of the goodness of life in spite of the sinister theologies into which they were born. From the outset their religion is one of union with the divine'.³⁶ These are the people who emphasise virtues like *courage, hope* and *faith*. Their religion looks out on the world and sees that it is good.

Sick religion, on the other hand, claims too much of evil as the very essence of life. People adhering to the latter, James writes, 'cannot so swiftly throw off the burden of the consciousness of evil, but are congenitally fated to suffer from its presence. Sick people are afflicted with the misery habit, the martyr habit'.³⁷ He coined the phrase *misery-threshold*. Healthy-minded people live habitually on the sunny side of their misery line, whereas the sick-minded live beyond that line in apprehension and darkness. And, to make his point vivid, he wrote that the healthy-minded seem to have commenced their life with a 'bottle or two of champagne inscribed to their credit' but the others are born 'close to the pain threshold', and the 'lightest irritants fatally send them over'.³⁸

A couple of decades ago, I tried itemising what, it seemed to me, were some of key characteristics of a sick religion. I then presented them in a lecture entitled Spirituality and Depression to a predominantly religious audience. The list included:

- a fearful view of a punitive God
- the giving away of self-determination by passive dependence on a dominant other: God, the Church, the latest guru, a partner
- a refusal to give credit to oneself for anything: all the glory has to go *up there* to God
- the repression of anger and any other feelings that are deemed to be bad or come under the strange category of negative
- a restrictive regime of moral shoulds that are the outgrowth of a highly idealised self

- a highly pessimist view of human nature
- a worried frown about the pleasure principle
- the **JO Y** acrostic: **J**esus first. **O**thers second. **Y**ourself last.

Since by the time of that lecture I had also done a big turnaround in my faith, I also listed what for me were some characteristics of a healthy religion, namely:

- an image of a God who is intricately connected to all of nature all the time
- a God who is in solidarity with human suffering
- a God whose first and enduring impulse is that of compassion
- a God who seeks to influence humans by means of persuasion, lure and encouragement
- a God who has a profound respect for human self-determination
- a view of human nature that recognises that the constructive lifeforce within the personality is at least as powerful as the destructive force
- a non-blame view of right and wrong
- a normalisation of human fallibility
- a recognition that this is a dangerous world and life can be unfair and unequal
- a validation of anger as a legitimate human emotion
- a portrayal of Jesus which does not minimise or deny his experiences of anxiety, anger, disillusionment and sadness
- a practice of prayer that does not implore an 'up there', 'out there' God to come 'down here' to perform some sort of miraculous psycho-surgery on our troubled emotions, a wonky marriage, cancer cells or an approaching tornado.

If I were to write a list these days, it would be modified somewhat. A different audience and changes in my thinking would account for this. I would also substitute the word neurotic for sick. Neurotic refers to behaviours and responses that are life-denying, restrictive, unadventurous, often compulsive and unexamined. A reasonable way, surely, to describe the religion of some, in part or full. By contrast, heathy-minded religion is life-affirming, forward-moving, adaptive, and person-centred. The colours of a healthy-minded religion are gold, green, blue, but accommodate black, red, and grey. By contrast, the primary colours of neurotic religion are black, grey, red with only a slight tip of the hat to green, blue and gold. Readers will have their own language to describe their religion. Labelling aspects or the whole of it as *sick* may not work well for them. They will find language that does.

One religious author who did stay with the language of sickness was Wayne Oates, Baptist theologian and pastoral counsellor. His book *When Religion Gets Sick* emphasised the possibility of public and private religion becoming dysfunctional. He took the view that religion is sick if it 'hinders the functions of life'.[39] A sick religion is one in which stumbling blocks and preoccupations cause major failures in functioning in specific situations for particular people.[40]

Then there is Sigmund Freud who wrote copiously about religion and none too favourably. His oft quoted sentence on the origin of personal religion is that 'God is at bottom nothing but an exalted father'. The desire for God arises from what he called 'infantile yearnings for a powerful, protective father'. God is an illusion constructed in the unconscious, a wish fulfilment. Lacking something deemed essential, individuals imagine a replacement, in the form of a strong friendly deity. 'God Creator is openly called Father.'[41] Given that my entry into religion matches this theory, I am a strong supporter of this viewpoint, but only as a reasonable narrative that helps explain the origin of religion for some not all.

An alternative psychoanalytic view to Freud's was proposed by a fellow Jew, Erich Fromm, who in 1934 fled Germany on the rise of Nazism to settle in the USA. Freud was to do the same from Austria to England in 1938. Fromm proposed an either/or view of religion. From the psychological point of view, he claimed religion can be one of two kinds: affirmation or escape. As an affirmation of life, it is an expression of an inner relatedness to humankind.[42] Religion as escape is a 'a reaction formation against a fundamental feeling of doubt'.[43] That is, unwelcome feelings of anxiety, doubt, helplessness are dealt with by overemphasising their opposites. Drawing on bravado and self-deceit, the individual pretends to be on top of everything. The dogmas of religion are an ally. They provide a safe refuge by means of which to combat the turbulence within. Another escape strategy, he claimed, is to flee to God. Surrendering to an external force will resolve all anxieties. Freedom and self-determination are too much to ask of themselves. Hand responsibility over to God. Fromm pointed out that his analysis explains only the psychological reasons for some people finding religion attractive. It has no bearing on whether there is a God.

So, there we are. This chapter has provided various perspectives that might be helpful to those in the later stages of life who are asking questions about how religion evolved for them and how well it served them. A prayer from Nikos Kazantzakis has relevance, highlighting as it does the view that defects in the religious experience lie not only in religion itself but in mindset of the one who is the bearer of that religion.[44]

The Kinds of Souls, Three Prayers

1) I am a bow in your hands, Lord. Draw me, lest I rot.
2) Do not overdraw me, Lord. I shall break.
3) Overdraw me, Lord, and who cares if I break.

Chapter 5

Has Christianity ever had to do a major U-turn?

Has the church ever got it wrong? Of course, it has; sometimes seriously so. There are numerous times at which it has disaffiliated itself from what it once vigorously promoted as the undeniable eternal true. Mind you, there is nothing novel or unique about that. Medical and legal professions have a similar track record of making major reversals in their belief and practice systems. Science too.

This section describes some of the historic U-turns performed by organised Christianity in its 2000-year history. The reasons for reminding ourselves about this? Simply to make the point that if the formal teaching authorities of organised Christianity have had to do J- or U-turns, then surely what's sauce for the goose is sauce for the gander. Pew sitters have a good precedent for making minor and major changes to their religious beliefs and their view of what is acceptable to the Christian conscience. In other words, if you are in the process of boldly doubting what you have previously been led to believe, you are in good company.

What follows are seven examples of U-turns undertaken by official Christianity in its 2000-year history. Some were major errors, but since everyone else on the planet thought the same way, Christianity does not deserve a fail mark for being part of universal ignorance. It was in good company.

No brownie points, however, to church councils for:

- obstinately resisting the new thing on the basis that the Bible teaches otherwise
- taking an awfully long time to admit its error, in some cases several centuries
- making changes to belief and practice only because not to do so would involve total loss of credibility with society at large and/or incurring unpalatable civil authority penalties
- for almost always being loath to say the *sorry* word after making the U-turn, perhaps reluctant to admit fallibility because to do so would compromise the credibility and authority of councils
- for alienating masses of enquiring minds with science-denying foolishness.

Lists of belief changes are not difficult to find. As conservative biblical scholar, Dr Bernard Ramm, wrote seventy years ago, many of the 'heresies' of former generations are now 'believed by all Christians ... many theories of science, once declared anti-Christian, are now accepted by millions of Christians with no evil effects on Christianity'.[45]

Dip into church history and it is not difficult to draw up a list of beliefs and practices which were once deemed unchangeable, non-negotiable, core truths, but have been repudiated as false or dubious and, in some cases, the source of terrible suffering for humans.

This chapter discusses several such beliefs:

- clergy gender: males only need apply
- marriage: definitely not for two people of the same sex
- planet Earth: immobile and flat
- dating the cosmos and humans: very, very recent
- the Second Coming of Jesus: imminent; could even be tomorrow.
- the geography of hell: down and awfully hot
- slavery: why not?

Clergy gender

It was unheard of in my early days as a young Christian in mid-1950s New Zealand that the ordained ministry would be open to women. Anglicans, Methodists, Catholics, Presbyterians, Baptists, The Churches of Christ, all shared the general worldwide opposition to – some would say repugnance for – the very idea.

The case presented seemed convincing. For a start, according to the Gospels, Jesus selected twelve males for his leadership team and zero women. Paul's view is also well known: 'In all congregations of God's people, women should not address the meeting. They have no licence to speak but should keep their place as the law directs' (1 Corinthians 14:34-35). Various other arrows were fired into the balloon that was floated in favour of female ordination, including one to do with hygiene. I remember a Presbyterian minister in a parish near to the one I attended in my teen years saying to me, 'Would you really feel comfortable receiving the sacramental bread and wine from the hands of a menstruating female?'

All this was the case in my experience sixty-five years ago in New Zealand. Suddenly, the watertight case began to develop serious leaks. First, the Presbyterians (1955) admitted women to the ordained ministry, then the Methodists (1959), and then the Anglicans (1977). World-wide, the tide began to flow this way. The unthinkable, the forbidden, the God-denying, became the valid, the acceptable, the God-endorsed. The illicit became licit.

But not everywhere, nor in all denominations. Roman Catholicism, for example, then as now, is implacably opposed to inclusion of females into the ranks of the priesthood. Even the occasionally progressive current Pope Francis has shown no interest in modifying the Vatican Position that the priesthood will never be open to women. The Roman Catholic church insists it has no authority to make any such change. They point out that Jesus gave the keys of the Kingdom to Peter, not to a woman, and chose twelve males and no females as his disciples.

Catholics are far from being on their own in this opposition to female ordination. Both Russian and Greek Orthodox churches ban it world-wide, as do various Pentecostal and Baptist Churches. The Presbyterian Church in Australia also introduced a ban on ordaining women subsequent to its continuance after the formation of the Uniting Church in Australia.

But many still work for change and believe in its possibility. WOW (Women's Ordination Worldwide), an ecumenical, international network, founded in 1996, is one example as it works with energy and hope for the admission of Roman Catholic women to the ordained ministries. Australia also has comparable women's advocacy groups. WWITCH (Women's Wisdom in the Church) is one of the twenty renewal groups that make up the Australian Catholic Coalition for Church Renewal, pushing for participation and equality of women across all levels of church hierarchy and ministry.

What we have here is a very recent U-turn, highly controversial, welcomed by some churches, banned in others. In other words, Christianity unable to come to a common mind. Rather reassuring for the bold doubter. If the religious hierarchy can't come to agreement on certain doctrines then, at the least, this is alerting the individual Christian to the fact that multiple choices are available when deciding what to believe on certain doctrines.

Marriage

Our next example takes us to a U-turn made by a national church on the issue of marriage, involving a complete reversal of a former strongly held viewpoint. No apology to those who had been wronged or even that a wrong had been done followed. Further, almost certainly, this dramatic U-turn would not have occurred had it not been for a change in Commonwealth legislation that directly affected one of its rituals.

What a time bomb the secular state threw into the boardrooms of institutional Christianity when, in December 2017, the Parliament of Australia legalised same sex marriage. The 'Challenge' was on. Predictably, official Australian Christianity dug in its heels.

Marriage is only possible, Bible endorsed, moral, God-blessed and wholesome if it is between a man and a woman. If you are both of the same gender, don't even contemplate such an illicit liaison, so contrary to decency and the Bible. As controversial boxing Champion Anthony Mundine put it on Twitter: 'My dad told me GOD made ADAM & EVE not Adam & Steve'.[46]

There was one denominational exception. Neither of the two biggies. One of the small ones declared *Let's do it*. The highest legislative court of The Uniting Church in Australia, the General Assembly, declared that same gender marriage could be endorsed. Two kinds of marriage were affirmed: a dual pathway. Each carried the same level of acceptability to the Christian conscience. Individual pastors and individual churches were now free to follow their Christian conscience in saying yes or no to gender inclusive requests for marriage. The Adam (male) and the Eve (female) marital prototype deemed within Christendom to be sacrosanct, and eternal, was now rejected as the only permissible way to go.

A dual track compromise was endorsed. A strange solution really, but a workable one. A re-affirmation of what once was, but a rejection of its exclusivity. Some thought this reasonable. But such a sweeping change was not acceptable to all members of that Church. A legal challenge by the NO party was launched and lost. Diversity had been endorsed. Tears of joy were shed by many. Tears of sorrow and rage by others. Dodgy politics, said others: the unity of the church is much to be desired in church politics, so find a middle path: two ways to marriage.

David Pocock, then Captain of the Wallabies, Australia's national Rugby team, had reason to be pleased. One of the greats of the game, widely acclaimed for his social activism and commitment to environmental issues, had made a pledge with his partner Emma not to marry until same sex couples could do the same. He said that 'we didn't want to join something all our friends couldn't if they wanted to'. When asked where these convictions came from, he replied that it definitely wasn't from his 'fairly conservative Christian family'. His values, he indicated, were more on building 'a society that is more just and inclusive'. Presumably, it were these same values that promoted him to become an Independent Senator in the Commonwealth Parliament.

As commendable as this policy is to the progressives within the Uniting Church, three questions still remain. If the Government hadn't set the ball going, would this change have been adopted? Why no apology to those countless couples to whom this traditional, one-track dogma had caused so much deprivation, anguish and disenfranchisement? And what strange religious mental gymnastics enables Church bodies to make a move from the implacable 'God is definitely not in favour of this' to 'God definitely likes this and supports it'?

Of course, the old way is still seen as the one true way by many in the world-wide church. For instance, in January of 2023, the Church of England released the results of a five-year consultation and debate on sexuality. A report presented to the Church's General Assembly proposed that the sacrament of marriage be restricted to a man and a woman. Same sex couples would not be eligible, despite the practice having been legal in England and Wales since 2013. The Archbishop of Canterbury did, however, indicate that if same sex couples did choose to access that marital right, then the church would offer them a ceremony of God's blessing.

Yes or No to planet earth as a mobile, tilted golf ball

Our third U-turn example is about a tide that turned on nearly all the Christian beaches of the world. And this almost universal religious self-correction is here to stay.

For three quarters of its existence – one and a half thousand years – the world-wide, official, Christian position about planet earth was that it was flat and structurally unable to move. If you travelled to its extremities, you would fall off its edges. Around this fixed planet the sun, the stars and the planets rotated. This geocentric (earth-centred) belief was also known as the Ptolemaic world view, named after the second century scholar Claudius Ptolemy, who adapted it from the Greek philosopher Aristotle.

Early Christianity did not invent this view of the universe, but had no qualms about endorsing it. Indeed, a flat immobile earth was taught in the Bible. What better authority could there be? It was the centre piece of God's glorious creation. Several stand-out Bible references – listed below – confirmed Ptolemy's science and Jesus, who was claimed to be the co-creator of the Universe as a member of the Trinity, put no question marks next to it while on earth for thirty-three years.

One stand-out biblical reference features Joshua, after whom one biblical book is named. Selected by Jehovah to lead the Chosen People into the Promised land, he is in hot pursuit of five resident Kings (Joshua 10:12-14). The sun is setting. With darkness approaching, it looks as though the residents will escape from the invaders. But wait! Joshua, strong believer in Jehovah's miraculous powers to aid him in this divinely- authorised military expedition, struts his stuff: 'Sun, stand still', he commands, and for good measure adds, '... and moon, you also'. At which point the sun, 330,000 times the mass of the earth, comes to a shuddering halt. Daylight is prolonged. The slaughter can now continue. And the story-teller concludes 'Never a day like it, before or since' (Joshua 10:14).

Modern Flat Earthers – Google them, if you doubt their existence – love this story. While on the Net, you will also be able to purchase a Flat Earth T-Shirt in various colours, sizes, materials, all soft and breathable and featuring a painting of a flat earth with a dome above, supported by pillars. Various Bible verses are quoted to support this cosmology, including Job 37:18, 38:13, Psalm 19, 1 Chronicles 16:30, Samuel 2:8 and, of course, Genesis 1 and 2.

The dramatic alternative to this flat earth scenario emerged most vividly in the middle of the sixteenth century. A Polish astronomer, Nicolaus Copernicus, published a book proposing that planet earth moved around the sun, not the other way around. Even more gobsmacking, the Sun was not only mobile, but sphere-shaped. Adapting to this sun-centred (heliocentric) view of our Universe was a big ask for both scientific and biblical scholarship of the day. Individual Christians and the Jesuits were open to this possibility, but certainly not the official church. If science and the Bible were in conflict, then only one of them was wrong, and it certainly wasn't the Bible.

Enter Galileo, claimed by some to be the father of modern science. Religious literature will more likely focus on his being declared one of the long-term heretics of Christianity. He was condemned as such and confessed to it on 22 June 1633. His heretical sin? That he was a sun centred believer. It took 350 years before the official church pronounced him no longer a heretic. On 3 November 1992, the then current Pope, John Paul II, admitted that in condemning him, the Church had got it wrong. He was no longer to be seen as heretical. He also added, however, that the church back there had acted 'in good faith'.

A recent highly readable biography by David Wooton[47] notes that a cluster of views led Galileo into trouble with the Church. He denied that God would make miraculous interventions in the natural order. He didn't believe in transubstantiation. He alienated the Jesuits, some of whom, early in the controversy, had found a way to give him support. His dealings with the Pope were less than diplomatic. His refusal to tone down some of his beliefs prompted some of that time to declare him a difficult and self-destructive personality.

But chief of his troubles was his declared support for Copernicus, which he (Galileo) presented in his book *Dialogue Concerning the Two Chief World Systems*. Nor did it help when he claimed to have found support for this theory by use of a telescope, the new scientific tool of that time, to which he had made significant improvements.

But it was the book that clinched it. In 1559, the official church had drawn up the *Index*, a list of books which Catholics were forbidden to read on the grounds that they were either heretical or against morality. In 1616, Galileo was warned by the Pope that he would be imprisoned if he continued to defend the Copernican view. Included in the *Index* was Copernicus's revolutionary book and in 1633 so too went *Dialogue*.

The inevitable happened. Galileo was summoned to Rome for his trial, arriving there in 1633. Though in poor health, and seriously in debt, he duly reported for the 12 April start to the hearing. Initially he took the line that he had *discussed* Copernicus in his book but not *defended* his position. Wootton writes that this 'cut no ice with Inquisitors, who had the document in their hands'.[48] Warned that he would be tortured if he continued to deny his Copernican view, 'Galileo gave way', as Wooton put it. That is, he confessed.

Sentenced to prison, he watched his book burnt in front of him. The Pope, at whose pleasure these issues lay, subsequently agreed that he could be held under house arrest and this was arranged with an Archbishop friend of Galileo's. After a brief time of residence there, permission was also obtained for him to return to his villa outside Florence, where he lived for eight more years. He died in 1642.

Time passed. Now, centuries later, a few religious Flat Earthers might occasionally get press attention for their case, but official Christianity has repositioned itself on the side of Planet Earth as a mobile sphere, a classic case of a decisive, official Christian U-turn.

Dating the cosmos and humans

Thirteen-year-old Sarah is on a school expedition, enjoying a hike among the fern and cypress trees of a Tasmanian forest. She stops at a colourful sign under a fern tree. It tells her that possums love to eat the new shoots of the fern and that 120 million years ago, dinosaurs dined on them too. This is not what Daddy says, she realises. He dates the world at six thousand years ago. The pastor of their local church says the same.

On the other hand, the chaplain in her school once said in Chapel that God did not give us the Bible to make us into astronomers or scientists. God gave us the Bible to make us Christians and scientists to work out the age of things. She thought that a good idea. She also tried to talk to her pastor about a ranger-guided fossil hunt on a local beach where the strange beauty of a former geological age excited her. The ranger claimed the fossils were over 300 million years old. The pastor agreed that they could be, BUT, he continued, when God created them 6000 years ago, God did it in a way that they seemed that old, but they really weren't. God did this, the pastor explained, to set up a test of faith in the heart and mind of the true believer: do you trust the Bible, or do you trust science? Sarah thinks this a strange thing to do and the explanation stupid.

The age of the cosmos and the advent of humans on planet earth have always been another of those hot potatoes for Christianity. But a U-turn it did make. Again, with difficulty, and slowly, and without apology. And it didn't take all of its constituents with it. My conservative Bible College of the 1960s proposed that 6000 B.C. was a ballpark figure to date the birth of the cosmos. They didn't tie it down to 22 October 4004 BC, as Bishop James Usher proposed, but they did favour that date for the creation of the first humans. The Thomson Chain-Reference Bible, so highly recommended in conservative Christian networks, does use this 4004 BC date, following Usher. A footnote proviso indicates that the date was to be used 'only as a working basis', and not be regarded as 'accurate'. This Bible does, however, date the Fall of Adam, as found in the creation story of Genesis, at 4004 BC.[49]

Much of ultra conservative Christianity – doctrinal Fundamentalism and Pentecostalism – still maintains that Genesis is an accurate record of what happened in history. This creating act was recent, not millions or billions of years ago. There was a designer and a creating agent: God. This is crucial because, in their view, life cannot emerge from non-life. Spontaneous creation out of nothing is an impossibility. Moreover, whatever was made was fully formed at the time of that creating act. As Genesis 1:25 put it 'God made wild animals, cattle, and all reptiles each according to its kind'. This is known as the fixity of the species doctrine and is irreconcilable with Darwin's position on evolution. Equally unacceptable to ultra conservative Christianity is the blackening of the Christian portrait of *homo sapiens* describing them as a product of the primate line. The biblical view is that humans are the crowning glory of God's creative acts.

But first world biblical scholars, including some Evangelical ones, are now not likely to blink if modern science says that the universe is around 14 billion years old. Moreover, say most of them, the theory of evolution is the best way to explain the appearance of human beings on planet earth. No big deal according to them for the God called Yahweh to take thousands, millions or billions of years to create something rather than to make it happen by the quick flick of the divine finger.

So here is U-turn of significant proportions illustrating, once again, the theme of this chapter that seismic faith changes are bound to occur in both personal and official Christian beliefs. Such modifications ought to be viewed as normative not naughty and regrettable. Hats off, therefore, to Cardinal John Henry Newman, for example, famous for the loved hymn *Lead Kindly Light* and also for a dramatic clergy shift from the Church of England to the Roman Catholic Church, who indicated that he did not have any 'great dislike or dread' of evolution. In just a decade after Charles Darwin published his *Origin of the Species*, Newman wrote this: 'It does not seem to me to follow that creation is denied because the Creator, millions of years ago, gave laws matter. He first created matter and then created laws for it – laws which should construct it into its present wonderful beauty and accurate adjustment of parts *gradually*.'[50]

And what about St Augustine (354-430 AD), sometimes dubbed an 'old earth' proponent, who suggested that God planted what he called 'the seeds of potential' in the world which were to unfold and grow in later ages. And Charles Kingsley (1819-1875,) clergy, novelist and social reformer, wrote about God creating 'primal forms capable of self-development'. He thought this was just as noble a conception of a creating Deity as the prevailing alternative explanations.[51] Then this from Frederick Temple, the Archbishop of Canterbury who, in 1884, argued that 'God did something rather more splendid that just make a world; he made the world make itself'.[52]

All of this is, of course, anathema to branches of orthodoxy. *Regrettably, this refusal resulted in many former adherents becoming* alienated from Christianity, both then and now. To put that another way, a sure-fire recipe for making children into atheists is for parents to set up a scenario in which their offspring are forced to choose between the Bible and science.

So much for issues about beginnings. But what about endings? At least two scenarios currently present themselves from the world of science. One is that, after the super gigantic Big Bang explosion, the Universe will keep on expanding for ever and ever. The other is that it will run out of steam and fall back on itself in an almighty self-destruct. The Big Bang of 14 billion years ago will become a Big Crunch in 5 billion years' time. Mainstream Christianity however has an entirely different take on the end time of the cosmos. To this we now turn.

Will Jesus come back?

Guess who is Coming Soon? read the bold sign in the window of a church-owned property right there on a busy main street of a famous coastal town, not far from where I live. I was intrigued. My mind sprang to two possibilities. One was Jesus. The other was *food*. I favoured the religious explanation, that the local people or their minister were making an attention-getting statement that the end of the world was imminent. Jesus would be 'back' soon. The none-too-subtle implication was that you had better be on the right side when that happened.

No hotter religious potato has existed in Christianity than the Second Advent. It is problematic, heated, organisationally divisive, a happy hunting ground for all sorts of weird and wonderful scenarios about how planet earth, and the universe itself, will be brought to a cataclysmic end. This belief that Jesus of Nazareth will come to earth twice, not just once, is re-affirmed every Sunday by hundreds of millions of Christians around the globe as they recite the following section of the Apostle's Creed: '... he will come again to judge the living and the dead'. Whether they believe what they are saying is another thing. Whether the celebrant believes it is also a moot point.

What is beyond doubt is that various Christian communities at different times and places have been seriously mistaken about this issue. Wrong about when the return will happen. Wrong about what will happen. And, as indicated, perhaps wrong in thinking that it is ever going to happen at all.

A little backfill about this issue is in order. There is no doubt that the Apostle Paul believed in the fact of Christ's return. Chances are some who are reading this right now have visited the Greek city of Thessaloniki. This town, then called Thermai, is most often associated with Paul's promotion of the idea that Jesus was to make a return visit to planet earth. At the time of his visit there, Thermai was a free, vibrant city, a trade centre built around a famous harbour, a meeting place of East and West. Little wonder that Paul went there to promote his new faith. Today, tourists still flock to this second largest city in Greece, also its second biggest port. Indeed, if you are interested in this sort of association, Rick Stein, British Chief, famous for his BBC TV series, also loves the place because of its rich gastronomic tradition.

There is little evidence that Paul was interested in the natural beauties or the menus of the place. His passion was Jesus Christ. Biblical scholars say he preached there for about three weeks around 50 AD, having crossed into Europe with the specific purpose of telling the Jesus story, as described in the 17th chapter of the Book of Acts. Apparently, he had to quit town in a hurry, not uncommon for him, though initially his message was well-received. A small community of new believers was established. Subsequently Paul heard not only good news about them but also something that alarmed him. He decided to write a letter to them. In fact, he probably wrote twice, some say only a few weeks apart, others considerably longer than that. The first is dated around 50 AD. Together they are known 1 and 2 Thessalonians.

The big problem was that some of the believers in this new faith community had become entranced with the joyous expectation that Jesus was about to make an imminent comeback. They were so spellbound that they had given up on their usual activities. Everything was on hold because of the marvellous thing that was just around the corner. Bible commentator William Barclay writes in his inimitable fashion that '... many of the Thessalonians ... were standing about in excited groups, upsetting themselves and everybody else, while they waited for the Second Coming to arrive'.[53]

It is worth reading these Thessalonians letters if you haven't already done so. In the first letter, Paul makes no bones about the reality of the Second Coming. He paints a vivid picture (1 Thessalonians 4:13-18). Immediately before his appearance, Jesus will be announced by the voice of an Archangel and a divine trumpet-call. He will then descend from Heaven. All believers who have previously died will be raised from the dead. Then, Paul writes, 'we' who are alive, will be taken up into the clouds along with the formerly dead and everyone will forever more be with the Lord. Setting out this timeline suggests that Paul was trying to be reassuring to those who were anxious about what would happen to their loved ones who were already dead. 'Don't fret' he indicates. They will be the first to get the call up, then, we will get the same. Scholars write that this use of we (first person plural), leaves no doubt that Paul believed that Jesus would be coming back in his own lifetime.

Each of these letters was meant to settle anxieties about end times. They were also an encouragement, spelt out in 4:9-12 of the first book, for the inhabitants to keep calm, to focus on daily affairs, to mind their own business and to work with their own hands. The punch line is business as usual, till Jesus comes.

The second letter uses more picturesque language in describing the events both before and during the revisitation of Jesus. One named as The Lawless One will appear, ushering in a reign of terror and rebellion. Signs and wonders will manifest themselves. Then Jesus will come with his angels in a flame of fire and those who are not believers will receive their just recompense: 'eternal destruction and banishment from the face of the Lord' (2 Thessalonians 1:9). As for that 'agent of sin', The Lawless One, 'The Lord Jesus will destroy him with the breath of his mouth'. Although written in Pauline style decades after the first one, some scholars suggest this letter way well not have been penned by Paul.

And here we are in the 2020s and Jesus has still not come back. Perhaps Paul's pastoral and pictorial efforts to stabilise an excited Thessalonian faith community did do what he hoped for. But it certainly hasn't put the brakes on extravagant Hollywoodesque, end-of-time Christian scenarios, not to mention filling libraries with books on what in theology is called the Doctrine of the Last Things. Believers in the Second Coming are not overly perturbed by Paul's getting it wrong about the timing of the event, given that some biblical scholars claim that most devout Jews of his time shared this expectation. The fact of it is what matters to them. It will happen and no one knows when. They also suggest there is evidence that Paul gave less credence to the Second Coming in his later writings. Perhaps so. What is also true is that some Christians give no credence to it at all.

It is certainly reassuring to some that no less a person than St Paul, the first great literary champion and travelling evangelist of Christianity, could be so wrong about something so big. Perhaps he made a J- not a U-turn by modifying only the timing of the appearance, not questioning its inevitability. Either way, he is a good role model for us. Faith changes are inevitable. Sometimes, they are substantial; at others, a modest tweaking is all that is required.

Back to the sign on the front lawn of that coastal village. Apparently, a parishioner asked the minister about it. Was it about

Jesus, or wasn't it? She seemed perplexed by the question. Eighteen months later, an upmarket, fast-food caravan was installed on the site. The sign was dismantled.

The geography of Hell

Famous American author John Steinbeck once travelled around the USA in a van with his poodle Charley. His gorgeous book, *Travels with Charley*, describes going to church one Sunday morning in Vermont and listening to a fire-and-brimstone sermon on a 'well-stocked, white-hot hell, served by technicians of the first order'. This Vermont God, he writes, put his sins into a new perspective. There was no room for the pally God of togetherness. It was all about Steinbeck as naughty child who was 'going to catch it'. He records that he put $5.00 in the plate, shook hands warmly with the preacher, and had a 'lovely sense of evil-doing that lasted clear through till Tuesday'.[54]

Hell gets considerable attention in the Bible, where it is variously described as a place of unquenchable fire, a pit into which unbelievers are cast, a 'place of misery' in which there is much 'weeping and gnashing of teeth'. Jesus also adds his opinion, once referring to 'the fires of hell' as appropriate punishment for wrong behaviours (Matthew 5:22; 18:9).

To understand the cosmic geography in biblical times, picture a three-storey bus. The top storey is the eternal dwelling place of the immortal God. The middle storey is Earth where mortals live. The bottom storey is hell, the furthest place from God. The *New English Bible* (p. 148) contains a visual graphic of this ancient cosmology.

For much of its history, Christianity accepted that hell was a real place. Even today, in the year of our Lord 2024 AD, Christians world-wide get to their feet in church on Sunday and say the words of the Apostles' Creed: '... he descended into hell...' Presumably not all of them believe in a vast, super-hot facility somewhere deep down beneath them. Nor do they necessarily believe Jesus made such an expedition, even if they are saying they do. But many in the past did believe in the place literally and that Jesus did make a visit there.

Scholars interpret this doctrine of descent in a variety of ways. Some say Jesus went down there in order to preach to the damned. Others that going there was a victory tour announcing the demise of Satan and his legion of nasty demons. Then there are those who interpret the phrase metaphorically. To say he descended to Hell means that he experienced the pangs of hell in his own body while on the Cross suffering on behalf of humanity.

Christian scholars eventually had to do some fancy footwork on the idea of hell as down there in the centre of planet Earth. How could they not, given the new cosmology promoted by science? Language about hell as a location was replaced with language about hell as an experience. Hell is redefined as a subjective state of suffering brought on by an irreparable relationship breakdown with God resulting in intense, permanent, mortifying grief and despair. John Calvin interpreted the Bible passages about darkness, weeping, gnashing of teeth, and the fires of hell, as figures of speech. These physical metaphors, he wrote, are used by the biblical writers to 'fix our thoughts upon this; how wretched it is to be cut off from all fellowship with God'.[55]

Then there are those who have done a full U-turn and joined the ever-growing crowd who say that the notion of eternal banishment in hell, designed by God as a consequence/punishment for disobedience, or for any reason at all, is downright reprehensible. None is more currently oppositional and appalled about this punitive deity than the Church of England theologian Alistair McGrath, currently Professor of Historical Theology at the University of Oxford. He quotes the sentiment of Robert Ingersol, American abolitionist of the nineteenth century, who famously stated that no one could believe in eternal punishment 'unless he has the brain of an idiot or the heart of a wild beast'.[56]

McGrath agrees with the criticism emerging from modern atheism that the doctrine of eternal punishment raises enormous questions about the 'moral character of God'. Everlasting banishment to this place or state cannot be reconciled with the modern concepts of 'decency and even-handedness'. He claims that atheism in our time arises mainly because such ideas and values 'are at least inferior to, and possibly irreconcilable with, the best moral standards and ideals of human culture'.

There we are. The U-turns keep coming. Another historic doctrine undergoing radical doubt and rejection, by some.

Slavery

Finally, a few words about slavery deemed an altogether OK belief in the Bible but now altogether not OK. Biblical scholar, Marcus Borg, whom I discuss later, wrote that there are several teachings found in the New Testament that 'tell us how some of our spiritual ancestors see things', but that they were not necessarily 'how we should see things'.[57] He gives three examples: the condemnation of same-sex relationships, the endorsement of patriarchy and acceptance of slavery.

Two snippets on slavery. In early 2022, Harvard University released a report which came clean on its involvement in the U.S. slave trade. The university detailed how its own faculty and staff had enslaved seventy people between the years 1636 and 1783. It also noted that many of the University's donors had made considerable money from the slave trade in the 17th to 19th centuries. Accordingly, Harvard decided to atone, committing $100 million to slavery reparations.

In March 2023, the *Guardian* newspaper issued its own public apology. Research had discovered that John Taylor, who launched the paper in 1821, was the owner of businesses involved in cotton which was picked in the field by slaves. Other *Guardian* financial backers also had links to the slave trade. The *Guardian* apologised to communities affected by slavery as well as to surviving descendants for this crime against humanity perpetrated on their ancestors.[58] The paper set up a ten-million-pound reparation fund to underwrite a ten-year program of restorative justice.

Everyone now seems to be apologising for slavery. The Pope, the Southern Baptists, the Prime Minister of The Netherlands, the Episcopalian Church of USA, Tony Blair (one-time Prime Minister of England), The Bank of England and various others.

How things change in 2000 years! Slavery in biblical and Roman times was mainstream. Now it is denounced as repugnant, contrary to the Christian doctrine of the intrinsic worth of each individual, and unacceptable to any reasonable social order.

Slavery is taken for granted in both the Old and New Testaments, never questioned as an inappropriate or morally wrong social practice. God is reported as being very, very unhappy about lots of things in the Scriptures – idolatry, pride, worshipping other gods, covetousness, infidelity – but not once about the owning and using of slaves. *Philemon*, the briefest letter of the New Testament, takes up slavery as its single issue, not to condemn the practice as might be expected, but to endorse it. In the letter, Paul is returning a runaway slave by name of Onesimus to his master Philemon, encouraging the owner to *take him back* not only as a slave but also as a brother. A tall order, one would imagine. Certainly, there is no derogatory mention of anything about slavery as an institution.

This is consistent with Paul's general teaching elsewhere in the New Testament: that slaves are to be obedient to their masters, and masters are to be kind to their slaves (Colossians 3:22 to 4;1; 1 Timothy 6:1ff and Ephesians 6:5-9). Paul even goes so far as to liken the obedience that the slave should show to the master as an analogy for the obedience believers should show to Jesus.

The always helpful *Dictionary of the Bible* edited by Jesuit John McKenzie writes this: 'It has always been a source of wonder and even of scandal that the NT seems to take a neutral attitude towards slavery, accepting it as a social fact'.[59] Even so, McKenzie's dictionary claims that 'historically, Christianity has been the only effective destroyer of slavery'. Perhaps so. Some agree.

Has Christianity ever had to do a major U-turn?

The name John Newton (1725-1807) often comes up in this context. In his hymn *Amazing Grace*, he describes himself as a wretch saved by divine grace. Perhaps, in part, this self-blame designation refers to his days as a captain of several slave-trading vessels before his conversion to Christianity and subsequent training as a clergyman. In time he became a prominent abolitionist, supporting the work of the Committee for the Abolition of the Slave Trade formed in 1787. A few months before his death, in 1807, the British Parliament passed *The Slave Trade Act* prohibiting the trade in the British Empire. Newton must have been enormously gratified.

Perhaps not all the British colonisers heard about this ban, including those who landed in Australia. Slavery has existed in this country in a variety of forms from 1788 to the present day. First Nations people were forced into servitude for no pay or had their pay stolen. Modern types of slavery in Australian include human trafficking, forced labour, child slavery, forced and early marriage and domestic servitude. According to the International Labour Organisation, as many as 15,000 individuals exist in these kinds of enslaved conditions in Australia. As a response to these trends, the *Modern Slavery Act* passed by the Australian Federal Government in 2018 required what it call entities to report on the risks of modern slavery in their supply chains and operations and to describe actions they have taken to address these risks.

Presumably, the Apostle Paul and his fellow Bible writers would have agreed with this had they lived in these times. Fortunately, what is morally acceptable in one era can become another era's sins. All credit then to the Australian Catholic Antislavery Network (ACAN) which has declared as its mission to 'Eliminate modern slavery in all its forms in the operations and supply chains of Catholic entities in Australia'. On 2 December 2015, World Day for the Abolition of Slavery, fifteen religious organisations gathered in support of the abolition of slavery and committed themselves to work actively for that cause.

We opened this section on slavery with Borg's sentiment that how the Bible writers – or any of our spiritual ancestors – saw things Is not necessarily how we see them or should see them. Religious turnarounds are inevitable. True for institutionalised Christianity. True for the individual believer.

Surely an appropriate way to close our chapter on U-turns by Christianity.

Chapter 6

Managing the doubt process

Is there a predictable pathway taken by those on the journey of doubt or disbelief? Probably not. More like a meandering river than an arrow going in a straight line to its target. A video shot would portray a trajectory curving this way and that, moving at various speeds, encountering a variety of obstacles, but on the whole, forward moving.

As with any change, the process is about intermingling rather than sequential phases. Each phase has its own challenges, tasks and rewards. Emotional intensity varies across the journey. Anxiety, anger or relief may be high in one phase, but entirely absent in another. Phases can also be concurrent. Fits and starts are common.

Each phase has its own time frame. Some are completed in a few months. Others take years. It is also possible to get stuck in any of the phases, making minute gains before moving on. And some come to a complete halt. They fail to complete the journey. The river is allowed to dry up. Psychology calls this arrested development.

Some individuals take this journey on just one or possibly a few specific issues. For many, it is an evolutionary journey that lasts a lifetime. Even in the last few hours of life, some make a surprising discovery.

As in all things dynamic, the personality of the doubter has a big say in how the process will unfold.

If you are looking for some clues about how to manage the doubt process, the following can help. First some broad bush suggestions. Then I suggest three options for working through doubt.

Seven brief broad-brush suggestions

Don't be intimidated by the religious dominators. Probably it is best to avoid them. These bodyguards of 'the faith once given,' can be super anxious about an individual's autonomous right to make sense of the Christian Gospel for themselves. Some of these minders, having once flirted with disbelief and been threatened by its arousal, swat the doubt away in a big-time defensive strategy and thereafter condemn whenever they sense it in others.

Hasten slowly. In a novel I recently read (the title of which I have forgotten), a grandmother says to her granddaughter, 'When making a change ... never be sentimental and always be swift'. The encouragement not to be sentimental sounds spot on when applied to changing a religious sentiment. Not recommended though the bit about being swift. Working through our doubts is seldom done in a hurry, does not need to be, nor can be in many circumstances. Besides, effecting changes to one bit may disrupt other bits, thus slowing the process.

Find a sage or two. A sage is a wise, considerate, compassionate other who can be helpful to those who wish to explore something for themselves. Finding such a person can be difficult. What you are looking for in the skill set required of a good sage includes – at the very least – a capacity to listen, a disinterest in promoting what you should believe, and the capacity to suggest pathways that might be worth exploring. There is an old adage in psychotherapy that the role of a therapist is to accompany the enquirer along the rough tracks of life, having also themself more than once traversed such a track.

Be prepared for a nugget of gold to remain. Sometimes what remains after a faith spring clean is both a surprise and 'a keeper.' Author and journalist Geraldine Brooks grew up a Catholic. She and her sister 'dragged themselves to Mass and went to a Catholic school.' The Nuns there, she reported, were dedicated to women's education and were a bunch of 'ardent feminists', which, she thought, was fantastic. But, in her words, she became 'incredibly pissed off by the fact that the Catholic Church was against birth control and the consequences of that stance for the developing world'.[60] As a result, she left, rebelling. But she took with her a social conscience, which she said was probably created 'by the same Nuns who I was rebelling against'. A worthy nugget!

Banish distorted God images. Mathematician and philosopher Alfred Whitehead (1861-1947) gave three examples: The Ruthless Moralist; the Imperial Ruler and the Unmoved Mover. Healthy-minded religion invites us to scrap these types of God profiles and go searching elsewhere. For encouragement, here is what American actor, Kelsey Grammer, once wrote: 'Just because you express doubts doesn't mean your faith is gone. It is worth expressing your doubt. God – or whatever you want to call It, Him or Her – will usually find a way to thank you for expressing your doubts'.[61] We would hope so! A God with whom we would land into trouble for changing some of our beliefs would be somewhat precious, surely. And since all language about God is symbolic, some find themselves settling for God images other than those where God is presented in the language of personhood – a Father, a Mother, a Friend

Mental laziness won't get you there. Gains are usually achieved by personal brain work. This involves reading on the subject you are troubled about and also having conversations with others. *If it is to be, it is up to me* is the buzz phrase that applies here. Albert Schweitzer wrote, 'I know that I myself owe it to thinking that I was able to retain my faith in religion and Christianity'.

Do a Descartes. This famous French philosopher wrote much about doubt and once gave what he called a homely example of how he went about dealing with doubt. Imagine a person taking up a basket of apples, he wrote, and fearing some of the apples might be rotten and infect the rest he resolved to tip them all out, then inspect them *singly and in order* and was then able to replace in the basket those that were not rotten. Apple inspecting. A helpful analogy for doing religious doubt.

Three options for working through doubt

(i) Just surrender
This is a simple requirement. Don't try to mega-manage the process. Just let the river of doubt pick you up and take you on a journey. There is nothing more to be said about this option. It appeals to some and works for them.

(ii) A three-step process
This section provides a threefold, step-by-step process in dealing with religious doubt.

The first step is developing clarity about the doubt. Doubts often emerge as shapes in the mists. Frank Sinatra, Ella Fitzgerald, Louis Armstrong, Sarah Vaughan and Billy Holliday have all sung about this. George Gershwin's 1937 song *A Foggy Day in London Town* offers a melancholic stranger wandering in pea soup fog on a London morning. Alone and consumed by self-pity, he wonders what to do. Suddenly he spies something in the mist. He stays with it. It turns out to be the luckiest day he could imagine. The fog dispels. The sun breaks through in the form of a special *her*.

Poets love this image of the fog or mist. It speaks to them of the latent, the hidden, the somewhat mysterious that sits in the background waiting to be seen and claimed. Psychology refers to it as the unconscious. Something is knocking on the door of our awareness: an unclear idea, an impulse, a memory, a feeling. This something is seeking full acknowledgment.

Religious doubts are seldom suddenly born in mature form. Their initial appearance is tentative, ill-shaped, unclear. They are inviting our attention. Sometimes our over vigorous door keeper has reasons for delaying or even preventing their access. What we can't avoid is that something is there, not nothing.

Perhaps some examples might clarify this idea of doubt or unbelief sitting unrecognised, unclaimed, un-owned in the mist:

- you feel disinclined to sing with your usual consenting gusto the words of an Easter hymn or say with good conscience some

words of the creed, but you don't examine what this hesitation might be telling you
- a church-related, social activity which once roused so much pleasure no longer does so. You are not sure why, but you note you are making excuses for not attending
- a doubt about a particular way of interpreting the Bible emerges, but is quickly silenced; perhaps it is replaced by an unpleasant anxiety or the opposite: a robust affirmation
- in a discussion with a long-term church friend who is moving to a new location, you notice your irritation about how confident they are that God will *lead* them to the best local real estate agent and the best house at the best price. Your irritation about this surprises you, but you don't explore the feeling
- increasingly, you find yourself feeling unimpressed by what the minister is saying in Sunday's sermons, but you don't explore the issue further
- a feeling of spiritual aridity begins to emerge. You tell yourself that it will pass, so best to press on regardless. Two years later, you are still in this same religious drought.

Not all doubt emerges in these ways. Some doubts come to our awareness with a reasonably clear profile. Regardless of how they appear or what they are about, the task at this point of the process is to give the doubt permission to clarify itself. Let it speak. This may require re-educating that sub-conscious doorman who specialises in holding things down. Doubt is not an alien, an intruder, a traitor, poor quality faith or the Devil getting at us. Doubt is a legitimate mental/religious activity.

Hold doubt in your open hand and let it speak. This is what step one is about.

The next step in the process is critical examination. Having gained clarity about what is troubling us, we then grant it the courtesy of a thorough investigation. What is the nature of the complaint? What defects are being alleged? Are they mild, moderate or severe? How legitimate do they sound?

Most religious doubts fall into one of two categories. One questions the believability or truthfulness of something. The doubter suspects that low probability now attaches to an event or idea that previously had not been questioned. The other type of doubt suspects that specific religious teachings about how human beings should behave are no longer valuable as a guide along the pathways of life. Worse than that indeed they can also be downright unhelpful, even dehumanising. These are legitimate existential doubts.

This phase of critical examination can also be conceptualised as questions in search of answers. Should we always tell the truth? Is it always wrong to accelerate dying? Did Jesus really raise Lazarus from the dead? Did Mary become pregnant by a divine miracle? How trustworthy are the Gospel narratives about what Jesus said? Are diseases and tornados sent by God as punishment for wrongdoing? Is Jesus returning? Is the dictum to always put others first reasonable? Is abortion the murder of an innocent? Does praying for rain really work? Can civil disobedience sometimes be endorsed by Christianity? Is the expression of anger sometimes justified?

Exploring these doubts requires active engagement, supplying your brain with new ideas. Take yourself off to the library. Let Google help. Buy a book or two. Browse a religious bookshop. Use the net to find workshops or courses on religious topics. Talk to trusted others. Perhaps begin a journal.

What also helps in resolving doubt is ridding the mind of the idea that there is only one good or true answer to any religious teaching. A rich range of alternative options is always available for consideration if you take the trouble to go searching for them.

A major hurdle some face in this part of the process is making changes to their view of the Bible. This Sacred Book of Christianity generally gives up its secrets in two ways. One is when the reader, like Jacob, wrestling all night with his angel, is prepared to lay down the challenge and wrestle with vigour. Part two of this book discusses how modern biblical scholars are doing a very commendable job trying to work out how the Bible was written and how best to interpret it. A $40.00 book purchase on this subject has much to recommend it. The Bible can also give up its secrets in response to an attitude of open listening. Receptivity has its rewards. Christianity commonly speaks of this as the imprint of the Holy Spirit. Some prefer to think of this as the sub-conscious breaking through.

Working through religious doubt will also require acceptance of unwelcome or heightened feelings. We can become frustrated by how long the process is taking, with no guarantee of a good result. Annoyance can emerge either at our own self for not having listened to the new voice sooner, or at others for leading us down a wrong path. Anxious feelings are common. Where might this doubt lead us? Some can even plunge into foreboding that there could be some nasty payback, a divine retribution for failure to trust in the good old-fashioned way.

Coming out is the last of our three-step process. Strictly speaking, there are two parts to coming out. The first is coming out to ourselves, which we have just discussed. Then there is the coming out to others. In liberal-progressive churches, owning up to others about our doubts and faith changes usually gets the tick of normalcy. In moderate to traditional congregations, a strong, unwavering faith is not promoted as the norm. 'We all have doubts from time to time', we are told. Nevertheless, some folk in those congregations may still be reluctant to voice their reservations about core beliefs, especially those to do with the Bible, God or Jesus.

On the far right of Christianity, doubt is not a good thing to admit to. Tolerance of doctrinal dissent can be low. Serious doubters can be labelled as backsliders, apostates, got at by Satan, or lacking in faith. Mini doubts may be tolerated but anything beyond that is naughty. Serious doctrinal dissent and/or departure from certain ethical norms can result in the offender being required to sit in the back row of the worship service for up to three months, or to attend classes to re-establish commitment to the core values and beliefs of that community.

Declaring religious doubt to partners can be tricky. In some cases, the partner may have picked up on your reservations before you do, or before you get around to telling them. And if you have been going to church as a twosome for decades, and find you no longer want to, your partner may not welcome your reluctance, especially if shared spiritual values have been a key linking thread in your relationship. Few in Christendom deem a partner's faith loss a necessary or sufficient reason to require a marital separation. But if they strongly agree with St Paul about not being 'unequally yoked' (2 Corinthians 6:14), renegotiating a new relationship contract may not be possible.

Declaring religious doubt with employers affiliated with Christian institutions – the local church, denominational structures, schools, hospitals, charities, community-oriented programs – may cause big trouble. This will depend on what is affirmed in the employer's mission statement; what the doubt is about and the doubter's level of seniority in the organisation. Potential penalties include warnings, limitations to career advancement, retrenchment, retraining, position relocation and more. Clergy in congregations or seminaries, as discussed in chapter seven, are especially vulnerable, if they come clean publicly and often, as also discussed in chapter seven.

How to say what about doubts and when and to whom can rob some of sound sleep. The anxiety is sometimes not what to say in the first place, but what to say in reply to a negative or hostile reaction. Preparing second phase comments can come in handy.

Coming out about religious doubts is, however, not always troublesome. Most outers are pleased to have persevered. Joseph Fletcher of chapter 3 is one example. He described how his own going public about his disbelief resulted in a feeling of keeping faith with himself and a welcome state of freedom and mental calm. True, there was little or no negative reaction in his case, but even those who encounter disapproval or worse often report that the gains outweighed the deficits.

(iii) A seven-step process.

The following will appeal to those who prefer a grand plan with lots of structure to the process. Basically, it is a breaking down of the three step into more detail.

Schematised, it looks like this:

- recognise that part of oneself is discontent about religious beliefs, values, practice
- give oneself permission to pay attention to it
- befriend it and clarify what it wants to say
- do solid homework on the stated problem; be alert to new insights, fresh formation, the solidifying of new patterns, and the stabilising of feelings about this process
- own the new as yours
- decide whether to come out to others, to whom and what to say. If you do decide for non-disclosure, stick with that until you decide otherwise down the track.
- give yourself a high five for the courage to change.

As good as it can be for some to come out about doubt, others find no need to do so. Similarly, some find no need to talk about what they do believe. Swede Dag Hammarskjold, diplomat and international peacemaker, Secretary General of The United Nations (1953-1961) belongs to the camp of the silent in regard to his Christian commitment. After his mysterious death in a 1951 plane crash, a journal was discovered with a letter of instruction to his executer concerning its publication. *Markings* became one of the famous pieces of 20th century spiritual literature, one which Hammarskjold described as 'a sort of White Book, concerning my negotiations with myself – and with God'. Nice phrase! Silent conversations and negotiations.

Admittedly, his story was about religious commitment not religious doubt, Perhaps prudence was a consideration, given the nature and world-wide scope of his work. Evangelical Christians who have an imperative to 'witness to Christ' will perhaps take the view he was letting the team down. My own view is that going public about what you do believe or what you certainly don't believe or what you are having troubling about believing is a horses for courses issue. Some will find it helpful and necessary. Some won't.

Chapter 7

Heresies, ancient and modern

Australasian clergy who took bold doubt too far to be tolerated?

One sunny 1965 Sunday morning in Florence's Piazza della Signoria, I found myself standing mute on the exact spot where on 23 May 1498, Dominican monk, preacher and reformer, Savonarola, was hanged and his body burned at the stake for treason and heresy. He had committed the heinous crime of disobedience to the Pope. I and a number of other visitors shook our heads in disbelief. We were familiar with capital punishment for crimes of murder or military desertion but being hanged for unbelief, and by your own religious employers, seemed more than a bit rough.

A seven hour drive north-west of Florence takes you the small village of Champel, just outside Geneva, the location of another execution for unbelief. Not by the Catholic Church this time, but by a reactionary off-shoot of it: Protestantism. Michael Servetus was the victim. Tried and convicted of heresy by the Roman Catholic church on account of his unbelief in the doctrine of the trinity and the divinity of Jesus, he managed to escape his Catholic condemners. Unfortunately for him, he took refuge in John Calvin's Geneva. In a complicated set of circumstances, the Civil authorities there also took unkindly to his falling short of doctrinal correctness, denying, as he did, not only the Trinity but also rejecting the rite of baptism.

Calvin's role in this execution continues to be debated, attracting censure for his failure to argue harder than he did for a less harsh form of execution. The upshot of it all was that on the 27 October 1553, Servetus was taken away to pay the penalty for his heretical views. Historian Roland Bainton describes how Servetus was led to a pile of green wood. A crown of leaves and straw sprinkled with sulphur was placed on his head. One of his own books was tied to his arm. His body was firmly attached to the stake by iron chains and a stout rope wound around his neck four or five times. The fire was lit. Servetus emitted an horrific shriek. As he lingered, more wood was thrown on the fire. In what Bainton describes as 'a fearful wail' he cried out: 'O Jesus, thou Son of the God Eternal, have pity on me'.

How fortunate we are, you might say, to be beyond all that now. To an extent, this is true. We certainly don't burn heretics these days. But heresy trials are still possible under that or other names. Some endorse them, claiming they are necessary, provided you don't overuse them. Others see them as monstrous. No place for them in modern religion they assert. In my fifty-five years as a minister of religion in New Zealand and Australia, two of my fellow Presbyterian or Presbyterian trained clergy were formally charged with heresy. Another was severely in trouble for being too public about his bold doubt. And other Australasian clergy during or before this time from other denominations either ran the risk of a trial or were subjected to one.

Occasionally, I played golf with one of them when he joined the Monday white ball hit-out of local clergy on a windy, coastal course in Dunedin, New Zealand. Reverend Lloyd Geering was the Principal at New Zealand's only Presbyterian Theological Hall and I was employed by him as a part-time tutor in Christian ethics and preaching whilst working nearby as a full-time parish minister. Two years before I took up that charge (1966), Geering had published an article in the national Presbyterian church paper entitled 'Is a New Reformation possible?' It was followed one year later by another titled 'What does the Resurrection mean?' Not for him the idea that Jesus was physically resurrected three days after his death. He thought it quite possible that the bones of Jesus could still lie somewhere in Palestine. It did not go down well in some circles. He then wrote four more articles clarifying his position, collected in a small volume. Other beliefs which he did not support included a 'literal inerrant Bible' the concept of the immortal soul, and the existence of a heaven to which believers went after death.

The controversy that resulted did not at first surprise him. But, as he writes in his memoir,[62] to be charged with heresy in the highest Presbyterian court in the land certainly did. Formal charges were brought against him by two litigants at the 1967 General Assembly of the Presbyterian Church of New Zealand. One charged him with 'grave impropriety of conduct' in teaching doctrines contrary to the Bible and The Westminster Confession. The other was a charge of 'gravely disturbing the peace and unity of the church by making statements which appear to be contrary to the church's teaching'.

Two days of the Assembly were set aside for the trial. On Friday, 3 November 1967, one thousand people packed out St Paul's in Christchurch. Television crews added to the drama. The *Auckland Star* noted that these charges were being heard exactly 450 years to the day since Martin Luther is alleged to have nailed his famous 95 Theses to that famous church door in Wittenberg.

On day one, the litigants presented their case and answered questions. Day two saw Geering present his rebuttal. After lunch, a motion was put, followed by a long seven-point amendment. A further two-hour debate was seen to be enough. The motion that 'The Assembly judges that no doctrinal error has been established, dismisses the charges and declares the case closed'[63] was moved and carried by an overwhelming voice majority.

Geering described how relieved he was. The unwelcome phone calls to his family ceased. Nasty objects were no longer mailed to him. He and his wife were especially relieved that their child was free of cruel comments from fellow students. But the doctrinal issue did not die down. Just the opposite. Divisions within the church worsened. One of the litigants resigned from the Presbyterian Church and started up one of his own. Some regular Presbyterian worshippers moved to other denominations.

Supporters of either or both of the litigants escalated their efforts for doctrinal correctness within the national church.

Despite being cleared of the title of a heretic, Geering was disappointed and saddened. He writes in his memoir that he had hoped the trial might have resulted in the Church 'giving a lead to becoming a Christian voice in society'. In his view, the Church was increasingly going backwards, thus 'failing to come to terms with modernity'. Little wonder perhaps, that in 1971 he took up a new position as foundation chair of Religious Studies in Wellington's Victoria University and soon became a prominent religious commentator. In 1988, he was honoured as Companion of the British Empire. At the time of writing (2024), he is alive at the age of 107, is now Sir Lloyd Geering and believes the defining issue of our times is climate change.

In April 2010, Geering came to Melbourne to give a lecture series at St Michael's, a downtown Uniting Church. Its Presbyterian trained minister, the Reverend Dr Francis Macnab, had also found himself having to respond to an action brought against St Michael's from the Synod of Victoria. In the foreground of the Synod's concern was a *New Faith* program which Macnab was conducting at St Michael's. Two issues were highlighted. One was that the public advertising campaign was deemed to be damaging The Uniting Church's relationship with other denominations and religious faiths. The second questioned whether the New Faith as promoted by Macnab was consistent with the doctrines of the Uniting Church.

Synod was not bringing a formal heresy charge against Macnab. Indeed, it couldn't. Unlike other Australian denominations, the Uniting Church in Australia had not included 'heresy language' in its constitution or discipline protocols when it adopted its *Basis of Union* in 1977. As we will see, however, the case has been made that some at the Synod took the view that Macnab had not only over-stepped the line in marketing his New Faith program, but that he also needed a solid reminder that, although the Uniting Church allows for a lot of grey in the preaching of its clergy, it is possible to take this freedom too far.

A little background on Macnab might be helpful before proceeding further. Born on 21 June 1931 of Australian farming stock in Victoria, Macnab was impressively credentialed in both religion and psychotherapy. He had completed the then mandatory two academic degrees necessary for proceeding to ordination, plus a Ph.D. from the University of Aberdeen in Scotland. His ground-breaking work on the interface between religion, psychology, and existential philosophy was subsequently published under the title *Estrangement and Relationships Experience with Schizophrenics* and was translated into several languages. He was also a registered psychologist.

At the time of his requirement to address the concerns of the Synod, Macnab had gained prominence in a wide range of fields. Serious psychotherapeutic works, prayer books, volumes of sermons and addresses, various contributions to current theological thinking, a novel here and there - all seemed to flow effortlessly from his pen. He was also a much sought-after international speaker and conducted various seminars across the Pacific in 1972 under the auspices of the World Council of Churches. He served as Chairman of the Victorian Branch of the Australian Psychological Society in 1974 and 1975 and in 1982 was elected president of the International Council of Psychologists. He was also the Founder and Director of a major Australian psychotherapy clinic, The Cairnmillar Institute in Melbourne and was recipient of the Member of the Order of Australia.

During the thirty-seven years from his Collins Street Uniting Church appointment in 1971 to the time of facing the Synod's grievances (2008), Macnab had overseen a declining attendance at worship of around 100 flourish to over 900. The place was abuzz with educational, mental health, social justice, religious ethics and spiritual programs. In his major study on *The History of the Australasian Churches*, Dr Ian Breward, Professor of Church History at the Uniting Church Theological Hall, Melbourne wrote of Macnab as 'one of the most influential liberals who combined the insights of Christianity and various schools of psychotherapy'. He wrote glowingly of Macnab for establishing the innovative Cairnmillar Institute for counselling and life education, and for 'restoring life to .... one of the largest inner-city Protestant congregations in Australia', unified, he wrote, by Macnab's 'charismatic personality and remarkable communication gifts'.[64]

Macnab was neither traditional/conservative nor even moderate in his doctrine. He often described himself as liberal. He declared from the pulpit, as reported in the daily press and on TV, that the Ten Commandments were harmful not helpful; that Jesus was not divine; the Virgin Birth was a myth; that the Resurrection of Jesus could not be seen as an historical rising of a dead man; the Bible could not be taken literally; that God does not engage in selective supernatural interventions for troubled humans, and so on.

But the 900 individuals who sat in the pews of that down-town church were not coming to hear what Macnab didn't believe. They were attracted by what he did believe. His was a message about how a progressive version of Christianity could enrich human experience. Like one of his favourite theologians, Paul Tillich, he was trying to relate the unchanging inner message of the Gospel to the ever-changing human situation. As he once put it, his preaching ministry at St Michael's had demonstrated that 'the great themes of biblical religion can find stimulating application in contemporary thought and behaviour'. His Sunday audience was always appreciative of his existential style interpretation of the sayings or activities of Jesus. His various books of prayers reflected this new language about God as Presence, the Source and Ground of Life and Jesus as the New Being. His outlook on issues such as divorce, voluntary euthanasia, sexual relationships, gender, and IVF were consistently progressive.

Like some ministers of that time, Macnab also came to approach the Bible through the lens of The Jesus Movement, a biblical scholarship initiative that was gaining currency in some sections of Christianity. Chapter eleven of this book is devoted to that new movement in biblical scholarship. Indeed, Macnab had admitted that the Christianity which the New Faith presented was highly controversial and a radical alternative to the profile of Jesus as contained in the historic creeds of Christendom and in the UCA *Basis of Union*. It was certainly not acceptable to most of the staff of the Uniting Theological College of that time, nor to the orthodox within the UCA.

Perhaps it was inevitable that Macnab's alternative to mainstream Christianity and his promotion of it in public, (widely sought after as he was on radio, in the printed press and on TV) would bring him into serious trouble one way or another with the official councils of the Uniting Church or with some group within it. And thus, it proved to be. On the morning of Monday 16 September 2008, Melbournian and Sydney residents woke to a provocative article about him – with photos – in the Melbourne *Age* and the *Sydney Morning Herald*. Macnab had launched a 'new faith for the 21st century' initiative, highlighted by a massive billboard on the Tullamarine Freeway which read: THE TEN COMMANDMENTS, THE MOST NEGATIVE DOCUMENT EVER WRITTEN. For reasons best known to himself, Barney Zwartz, the Age Religion Editor of that time, had decided to bring this issue to public prominence.

Loud alarm bells sounded in the Synod office, then located across the road from St Michael's. The Synod of Victoria felt that an official reply was immediately called for. The Acting Moderator, the Reverend Sue Gorman, responded the very same day on the Synod website and with a communication to all Synod clergy, expressing regret for any hurt this declaration might have caused both within the Synod or to people of other faiths. Potential damage to inter-faith dialogue was high on her agenda. She reassured readers that no Synod money had been used in the Macnab promotion. She also drew attention to relevant material in the USA *Basis of Union* and authorised The Reverend Chris Mostert, Professor of Systematic Theology at the Uniting Church Theological College, to make a theological response which was attached to her communication. He amplified her reference to the *Basis of Union* and indicated that Macnab's public view about God and Jesus fell short of classic creeds about them. He also emphasised the importance of 'respectful and constructive relationships' with people of other faiths.

One week later, the Seventh Meeting of Synod of Victoria was held at La Trobe University for its annual four-day business program (21-24 September). The minutes of that meeting indicate that on Tuesday the 23rd, the Macnab issue surfaced on the floor of the Synod. A resolution was passed that the Moderator and the General Secretary convey to the Council of the St Michael's church its 'deep concern' at the 'offence' given to many Christians, Jews and Muslims by the signs and other media used in the New faith program, and the 'potential damage to ecumenical and interfaith relationships'. The Synod also requested that the offending signs and other media materiel be forthwith removed and an apology issued for any offence caused.

In order to process this business of the Synod, the Moderator, Reverend Jason Kioa, was commissioned to meet with Macnab in the church office on the third floor at 100 Collins St., Melbourne. This occurred in due course. Kioa also invited The Reverend Sandy Yule, Secretary of the Assembly Christian Unity Working Group, to be part of the discussion process. Eleven months later, after three separative interviews with Macnab, they filed their report with the Standing Committee of the Synod.

Meanwhile, much was happening about the issue both inside and outside the wider church during that time. One week after the Synod resolution, Barny Zwartz who also attended that Synod meeting did a 22 September follow up article sub-titled: *Gentle rebuke over minister's new faith*. He proposed that the Synod had come as close as it could in naming Macnab a heretic without having a disciplinary hearing. He noted that Reverend Kioa had put doctrine on the floor of the house when he told the Synod that Macnab's expression 'new faith' 'appears to be outside the teachings of the One Holy, Catholic and Apostolic Church'.

He also declared that Macnab's views as expressed in the media discarded 'much of what has been accepted for 2000 years as orthodox Christian belief'. Then three months later, just before Christmas, Zwartz published a third and final piece in *The Age (Melbourne) Magazine* entitled *Caped Crusader* further fuelling the discussion in the community at large as well as within the congregations and echelons of the Uniting Church.

Zwartz, an accomplished theologian himself, was not alone in proposing that Synod was not only concerned about Macnab doing damage to inter-faith and ecumenical relations, but also about his departure from acceptable doctrine. *Crosslight*, the official Uniting Church magazine, also carried articles (2009) which accused Macnab of heretical views. Former Uniting Church minister, the Reverend Dr Dorothy Lee, for example, wrote an article under the title *An old heresy in the guise of a 'new faith'*. In the same issue, a media view expressed by religious journalist Alan Austin indicated that Macnab 'may or may not be guilty of heresy', but it was not acceptable that he 'accuse Kioa of defamation' when the moderator raised with him the issue of 'orthodox teachings'.

Readers may be surprised at this *defamation* word. Macnab was, however, not the first or last to contemplate or threaten this response in defence of a charge of departure from the doctrines of the church, as our next case also illustrates. Those who knew Macnab well do not for a moment doubt he would have followed this course had the matter of departure from traditional doctrines been pursued further. But he did not take this course nor need to. He took the sign down, indicating it was only ever intended as a short-term publicity measure aimed at attracting more attendees at St Michael's and he also expressed regret at any unintended offence to the Jewish religious community.

Several months passed. The controversy slowly abated. Then in August 2009, The Reverend Kioa presented his report to the Standing Committee of the Synod. 'We recommend,' he wrote, 'that the Synod of Victoria and Tasmania take no further action with respect to the "New Faith" campaign of St Michael's'. The tone of the report was positive, almost irenic. Kioa and Yule indicated there had been three meetings with Macnab canvassing several topics. These included the intentions of the New Faith program; the concern of the church about schism and apostacy; theological issues such as the doctrine of God and Jesus; the expectation the church of its ministers as spelled out in ordination vows.

They were assured Macnab had no intention of establishing a new church, indeed that the new faith phrase best summed up his own spiritual and intellectual journey and that the program was orientated mainly to recruiting new members to the St Michael's congregation. They also indicated that congregations of the UCA need to be entrusted with 'a high degree of autonomy' in their life and work; that various interpretations of the Christian Faith will exist in the Church and indicated the need for 'more intentional engagement between strong congregations and the wider church'. In short, in my view, Kioa and Yule produced a healing document nearly a year after the heat generated by the initial stimulus.

Some say this was 'a welcome result'. Others breathed a sigh of relief, claiming that the Synod would have become the laughing stock of secular society had it pursued and censured him for departure from the traditional Christianity. Hardly a good look in the modern era with its societal themes of inclusiveness and tolerance. There was some speculation as to the reasons for the UCA going so hard and so quickly. Another Australian example of cutting down the tall poppy some suggested. More personally, it was suggested that Macnab had too much narcissistic 'me' about him, wholly unacceptable for a practising clergyperson. 'An asset grab'. suggested others, aimed at replacing Macnab with someone more Synod-friendly and thus bringing the considerable wealth of that congregation under its umbrella. And just where and how did he find those one hundred and fifty thousand dollars to promote and conduct that New Faith program some asked.

Then there were those who saw the whole thing as an aberration, an unfortunate event. 'An unlucky man' they said, for

Macnab to have to go through this in the first place, given that the Synod meeting of that year probably had a greater number of voting representatives committed to preserving the doctrinal purity of the Church. Zwartz had his own take on this when he wrote in his *Caper Crusader* article that the Synod meeting had been 'stung by the anger of conservative delegates',[65] meaning, presumably, that it was time to clip Macnab's all-too-liberal wings. Senior Synod officials of that Synod meeting continued to stress that repairing damage done to ecumenical and inter-faith relations was the concerning issue, not departure from doctrinal standards.

As for Macnab, he continued promoting his version of Christianity, writing more prayer books, publishing more of his sermons, producing large works on stress reduction, ageing well, and brief psychotherapy, doing his regular morning meditation, managing two large organisations and continuing on as Patron of the British Bulldog Club in Vic. He retired on Christmas Day, 2016, after 45 years in this one appointment, probably giving Synod cause to breathe a sigh of relief. He died on 27 April 2023 at the age of 91.

A brief footnote to this Collins Street saga. If you are inclined to the view that bad energy can be associated with a certain geographical spot, which I am not, you might be interested in the following. Directly across the road from Macnab's St Michael's is Scots Presbyterian part of the Continuing Presbyterian Church which had elected not to go into the union of 1977. In the 1880s, one of its ministers, the grandfather of a friend of mine, had also been tried for heresy.[66] In this case, he was found guilty and declared no longer to be a minister of the Presbyterian Church. The Reverend Dr Charles Strong was a Scottish born preacher educated in divinity at Glasgow. He had incurred the displeasure of his hierarchy for his liberal theology. Like Macnab and Geering, he was seen to have fallen short of required creedal correctness, particularly in his disbelief in the deity of Jesus Christ, the doctrine of the atonement and the bodily resurrection of Jesus.

Nor did it help that Strong was a crusader on behalf of the poor in Melbourne and was a critic of capitalism, not good themes to espouse in this inner-city church attended by the wealthy of that city. He was an activist in areas such as prison reform, village settlements, feminism, child care and justice for Aboriginal people.

Instructed by the Presbytery to change the tenor of his preaching, he resigned his charge, but was persuaded instead to take six months leave of absence. On returning from Scotland, he ran into more trouble for supporting the Sunday opening of the Public Library and the Art Gallery. He had also refused to disassociate himself from a public lecture on the relationship between science and religion given in Melbourne by Mr Justice Higginbotham who had declared that 'Creeds were the most insidious enemies of the religion of Christ'. Enough was enough for Presbytery. Strong was charged with 'promulgating and publishing heretical and unsound doctrine'. Not least of his derelictions was his failure 'to give prominence in his teaching to the Incarnation, the Atoning Life and Death, and the Resurrection of our Lord'.[67]

He again resigned and made plans to leave Australia, refusing to attend a meeting of the General Assembly to affirm his orthodoxy. On 15 December 1983, he sailed to the UK. The following day, the Assembly declared him no longer a minister of the Presbyterian Church. One year later, Strong returned to clergy duties, this time accepting the charge of the Flinders St Australian Church which, in time, he built to a 1000 strong community. But its decline over the following years saw him in 1992 assume duties as minister in a new and smaller building in Russell Street, just down the road from Macnab's church. He was to die in Lorne after a fall in February 1995 at the age of 97.

Our next case of an Australasian clergy formally charged with heresy (departing from the doctrines of the church) carries the dubious honour of being found guilty of the offence. 'Incredulous', writes social commentator Hugh Mackay, 'that such a thing could happen in the dying stages of the 20th century'.[68] But it did. I never met this clergy contemporary of mine, the Reverend Doctor Peter

Cameron, but read about him while serving in a Victorian parish. *The Age* covered the case with a full, front-page photo of his face under the tile *The Face of the Heretic*. *The Australian* headlined its surprise at the decision with *Heresy Finding That May Haunt the Church*. *60 Minutes* carried the story; Terry Lane did a half hour ABC radio interview with Cameron and Ray Martin introduced him on the Midday Show, declaring that although the program had featured high flyers, hookers, hypnotists and hawkers, 'this (was) the first time we've had a heretic'.

If reactions outside the Christian community were bemused or incredulous, not so within the Presbyterian church which brought the formal case against him. Various analogies were used to justify the heresy charge. One Presbytery official indicated that 'Dr Cameron has signed on to the Presbyterian church and has to play the game the way the Presbyterian church plays it'.[69] It is like joining a soccer club, he continued, then deciding to pick up the ball and play Rugby Union half-way through.

Cameron had come to Sydney in 1991 after two Presbyterian appointments in his native country of Scotland. He was first a parish minister at St Phillips, Edinburgh, for three years, then from 1987-1990 a lecturer in the Theological Faculty at the University of Edinburgh, where he had been a student eleven years previously. He had also studied music, law and completed a University of Cambridge doctorate. In 1991, he arrived as a well-credentialed scholar to take up his new job as Principal of St Andrew's College at the University of Sydney.

What then went wrong and so precipitously? A number of things, all of them discussed fully in his own book about his trials, entitled *Heresy*. For starters, he was unlucky (read unwise) to have joined the wrong stable at the wrong time. His initial mistake was joining up with the New South Wales Presbyterians who had voted not to proceed into the 1977 newly-formed Uniting Church. Cameron admits that he been warned that among those continuing NSW Presbyterians were some known as the Flat Earth Brigade.

In June 1992, he gave the address at the Jubilee Service to the Dorcas Society, the topic being The Place of Women in the Church. It was attended by 300 women and a handful of males. It was nothing short of a red rag to a bull. Here he was supporting a position which nine months previously, in September 1991, the General Assembly of the Australian Presbyterian Church – the highest court in that Church – had declared unacceptable. In a majority decision, it announced that the ordination of women was unbiblical, thus reversing a decision of seventeen years previous. But this was not all. Cameron's speech also declared in support of homosexuality, a further undermining of the authority of the Bible in the minds of the Church authorities. Cameron claimed that Paul's judgments were not binding: 'It's not simply that his views are time-bound, it is actually possible that he got things wrong'.[70]

No surprise then that within two weeks an official complaint had been lodged with the Presbytery. Due process was followed. Preliminary, unfruitful discussions with him led, unsurprisingly, to Presbytery's deciding to proceed with charges against him. What followed was a long, drawn-out saga which lasted for over a year and involved thirteen separate meetings. Complaints about his beliefs by individual clergy to the Presbytery turned into discussions followed by preliminary hearings and eventually to a trial.

On the 18 March 1993 at 7 p.m., a couple of years after his appointment to the position, the trial began at the Presbyterian Theological Centre in Burwood, Sydney, where the Presbytery usually met. It lasted for four and half hours, after which Cameron had been found guilty of the charge that he had made statements in his Dorcas Jubilee address inconsistent with Chapter 1 of *The Westminster Confession*, in which the key issue of the infallibility of the Bible was affirmed. The vote was 26-13. A further charge that he had made statements in the same address that were inconsistent with the teaching of the Bible on homosexuality was dismissed.

Cameron reports that his initial reaction was 'a mixture of incredulity, amusement and apprehension'. Before the trial, some of his supporters had encouraged him not to fight the charges, but to resign from the Presbyterian Church. This was not his style. He indicated that he would appeal the conviction to the General Assembly of the New South Wales, which he did, but lost after a hearing of over eighteen hours on the four days between 30 June and 3 July 1993.

Once again Cameron fought on, indicating he would appeal to the highest Court in Australian Presbyterianism, The General Assembly. He continued to reject the pathway of resignation, a course some had encouraged. He also rejected the notion of taking the issue to the civil courts to request either a review of the proceedings or to issue a defamation action. His belief was that that neither action was likely to succeed. He also refused the advice of some to switch to another denomination more sympathetic with his beliefs, The Uniting Church, for example. By the end of that month, however, he had resigned. In 1996, he returned to Scotland, eventually leaving the Church of Scotland and joining the Scottish Episcopal Church (Anglican).

On an ironic note, Cameron observes that perhaps he should have paid more attention to what he knew to be true, that he was not the first Presbyterian clergyman in that place troubled by charges of departing from orthodox beliefs. One concerned the Reverend Samuel Angus, Professor of New Testament at the NSW Theological Hall from 1914-1943. He was never formally charged with heresy, but for over a decade his departure from orthodox beliefs such as the virgin birth and the physical resurrection and ascension of Jesus attracted the attention of both the NSW and national Presbyterian jurisdictions. Perhaps his portrait by Jerrold Nathan did catch Cameron's attention, given that it hangs in St Andrew's College, where also a memorial lecture hall is named after him.

Not only the Presbyterians had this predilection for uncovering and denouncing doctrinal dissent. The Methodists were into it too. In a strange twist of fate, one of them, the Reverend Fred Noffs, who himself was to be on the receiving end of a heresy summons, was also fervent in condemning Angus. Enter the his biographer, Phil Jarratt, who notes that in Noffs' early twenties he had signed up with the Fundamentalist Methodists of that time in denouncing the 'dreaded modernists', of whom Angus was one.[71] Noffs' own trial was brought in 1976 when he had to answer the charge of 'unfaithfulness to the doctrines of the church,' or 'heresy by another name,' writes Jarratt.[72] Like Geering, Noffs was acquitted. 'The case was not proven', reported the committee that had reluctantly heard it.[73] But, as in Geering's and Macnab's case, the secular press made much of it: METHODIST MINISTER ON HERESY CHARGE blared *The Australian*.

As in our previous cases, support flooded in for the one who was charged. Professor Charles Birch, soon to become one of Australia's famous scientists, put a novel twist to the Noffs case. At that time, as Vice-president of the World Council of Churches, church and society departments, he expressed the view in *The Australian* that heresy was the 'life blood' of the church and 'the beginning of wisdom'. The Church should encourage heresy. How tragic to try to stifle enquiry and free discussion 'into the dogmas and creeds Christians have mouthed for so long.' 'Why', he declared, 'Heretics have always been vital to the church – Jesus was a heretic himself.'[74] Noffs would have whole-heartedly agreed with that.

My theme in this section has been the danger in which ordained persons in organised Christianity place themselves if – too often, too strongly, too publicly – they dissent from certain historic doctrines and/or engage in public activities deemed to be against church unity or good relations with sister religious faiths or in any way that brings the institution into disrepute. Their stories certainly raise the legitimate issue of how much dissent from the creeds ought to be allowable for ordained clergy in recognised ministries. How far should the limits of toleration be permitted to stretch in matters of doctrine? The orthodox do not allow for much at all. The moderates and progressive are open to a great deal.

A few further words in conclusion about this troublesome cluster of ordained clergy. All were evangelical in the true sense of that word; they were tellers of good news. They were not atheistic destroyers doing some demolition job on Christianity. They believed in grace and forgiveness; a compassionate deity; the centrality of Jesus; the fallibility of human beings; the possibility of a fresh start and in building constructive human communities. Each in his own way was intent on relating the enduring truths of the Christian message to the changing realities of each new era.

Their alleged transgression was not sexual or financial, but departure from what was deemed central to the belief structure of their employing body. Chief of these dogmas were the nature of the Bible, the divinity of Jesus and his resurrection.

All held what were deemed to be prestigious appointments. The organised church which eagerly prosecutes failures to conform in doctrine seems generally to be uninterested in the minnows in the lake, only the big fish.

All refused to renounce their doctrinal aberrations and reform their ways. All stuck to their guns through the lengthy public and in-house investigations of their belief systems and the colourful mileage the daily press made of the heresy accusations.

All finished their clerical careers so much more disillusioned with the organised church than when they entered it, continuing to be employed by the church. Five of the six continued to do what they were doing prior to facing the charges levelled against them. Only Geering gave away working in the church.

None of them crossed into atheism or at least none has declared this to be so. All seemed to be hell-bent on saving Christianity from itself. And probably all of them would agree with the sentiment of the Harry Emerson Fosdick, progressive USA Protestant clergyman who, when he found his way out of the rigours of a heresy charge, observed that he 'would feel ashamed to live in this generation and not be a heretic'.[75]

It certainly looks as if several stars have to align for such upheavals to happen. You must be a prominent person. You must be stretching the limits of doctrinal compliance. You must also be disinclined to back down or go softly. You will not be put off by first, second or even final warnings. You will be an on-the-front-foot personality type when in conflict. You will have no trouble being articulate, almost certainly be well read, and probably gifted. Perhaps you carry unresolved inner conflicts in relation to authority figures. Very likely you might be ambivalent about a centralised church bureaucracy. Also likely is that you would have risen high in whatever profession you chose.

Part 2

The revitalisation of Jesus studies

Chapter 8

The challenge to orthodox views about Jesus

Save Jesus read the sign on the brightly-lit notice board of the inner-city church located on a very busy intersection in Melbourne, Australia. 'Surely they got it wrong', a traditional worshipper might have said. 'Isn't *Jesus Saves* what it is all about? Perhaps the verger messed up. Hope he won't get into trouble'. But he didn't get it wrong and he didn't get into trouble.

Upstairs in the vestibule, a glossy pamphlet promoted an upcoming public program outlining how Jesus does indeed need to be saved. His time has come to be liberated from the whole cluster of misleading titles, identities, categories, personality attributes and powers which have been falsely attributed to him.

This was no atheistic attack on Jesus. It was conducted by a believer, a minister of religion of a mainline denomination and a public fan of Jesus. Nor is there anything novel about this sort of project. Getting rid of so-called false images and identities attributed to Jesus of Nazareth and re-presenting him with what are claimed to be more authentic and contemporary ones has a long history. Some were radical revisions. Others tinkered on the fringes.

Revitalisation, resurgence, renaissance are the words many modern biblical scholars use to describe what has happened in Jesus studies over the last two hundred years. They agree that Jesus did exist. They also agree that the name Jesus is legitimate. His mum, dad, siblings and everyone in his Palestinian village would have called him that. But the revisionists are unhappy about some of the other names given him in much the same way that some modern women do not want to take on their partner's family name since it defines them in a way that is for them unacceptable.

Over the centuries, an impressive suite of names and qualities has been bestowed on Jesus by the teaching authorities of the church and its biblical scholars. The question is, which of these identifiers would Jesus have agreed with? Here is such a list: God incarnate, a Jewish sage, a disillusioned revolutionary, the best of all possible humans, truly God and truly man, a phantom, a Man for Others, the Sacrificial Lamb, The Light of the World, The Messiah, Lord, a Prophet, Christ, the Anointed one, the Son of Man, misguided martyr, God of God, Very God of Very God, Master, a heretical rabbi, the Mystical Light, Teacher, Rabbi, subversive Sage, Envoy of Sophia, the inner wisdom, radical activist, Love incarnate. And this for starters!

How conflictual they are! They can't all be right. Many seem good contenders. But to whom and for how long? The troublesome truth is that Jesus himself was curiously silent, almost evasive, on any definitive identity statement. The Gospel of John records him as uttering a battery of *I am* (self-identity) statements, but many current biblical scholars, for reasons I will explain shortly, doubt they were actually uttered by him. When Peter had the temerity to declare to Jesus that he believed him to be the long-awaited Messiah, the response by Jesus has intrigued biblical scholars ever since (Mark 8:27-33). In fact, in biblical studies, it is discussed under the title of *The Messianic Secret*. Jesus makes no direct confirmation that this is how he also sees himself. More than that, Jesus gives Peter and the rest of the followers 'strict instructions not to tell anyone about him' (v. 30).

Did he or did he not see himself as the much longed-for Messiah? According to Jewish lore, the true Messiah would declare himself only very late in his ministry. Did he therefore accept he was the Messiah, but postponed the announcement? Orthodox scholars insist he was the Messiah and that he knew it; the biblical references that support these claims are trustworthy.

By contrast, German scholar Gunther Bornkamm is typical of many in mainline biblical scholarship in asserting, 'This is the truly amazing thing ... there is not one single certain proof of Jesus claiming for himself one of the Messianic titles which tradition has ascribed to him'.[76]

Nor does it help that outside the Bible there is scant evidence concerning Jesus from his own times. First or second century references about him by Jewish historian Josephus, by Roman historian Tacitus plus a couple more are claimed by orthodox believers to confirm that he walked the valleys and deserts of first century Palestine attracting many to his prophetic message and that he probably took the occasional dip in the Red Sea. In short that Jesus was as real an historical figure as Emperor Nero, or Charlie Chaplain or Gracie Fields! Atheists are not so sure. Bertrand Russell maintains that 'historically it is quite doubtful whether Christ ever existed at all',[77] though Richard Dawkins, that most forthright current critic of Christianity, is prepared to concede that he 'probably existed'.[78]

I was first introduced to this intriguing debate about Jesus' identity seventy years ago when I was a nineteen-year-old student at The New Zealand Bible Training Institute in Auckland. I wrote a final year exit essay on three of the many so-called heresies about Jesus in the early Church. Antinomianism was one: *anti* in Greek reads *against*, and *nomos* as *law*. A big theme of that Christian antinomian sub-group is that Jesus liberated believers from obligation to the moral laws of Moses. The downside of this conviction was that this claim to freedom morphed into lawlessness and was condemned accordingly. However, the profile of Jesus as a revolutionary figure challenging abusive authority of any kind has continued to find favour in various expressions. My second heresy *Docetism* – from the Greek word *to seem* – claimed that Jesus did not have a corporeal body while on earth. He only *seemed* to. His was a phantom body. Docetics stressed that no deity could ever take on the flesh of humans or suffer in any bodily way.

The third heresy was *Gnosticism* derived from the Greek word *gnosis* – knowledge. This movement pre-dated Jesus but claimed him as one of their wisdom teachers whose task was to point to the knowledge that liberated spirit from matter. According to them, Jesus did not die nor needed to die in order to achieve salvation for others.

Credit then must be given to my very conservative Bible college for exposing me to these various erroneous options offered so soon after his death, and to the question he himself posed, but would not or did not answer, 'Who do people say that I am?' Mind you, I would not have been admitted to that conservative Bible College had I believed any of these three, or any of the other numerous such 'heresies' that surfaced in the early church. A fundamental prerequisite for admission to College was to believe that Jesus was the divine Son of God, fully God and fully human, the sin-bearing Lamb, my personal Saviour and Lord. This view was the only true and acceptable identity package. At that time, I had no hesitation in complying. They seemed then undeniably true.

Initially, it fell to leaders like Paul and Peter to rebut what they believed were the false conceptions that soon emerged within some of the early house church communities that sprang up after Jesus' death as recorded in the Book of Acts and the Epistles of the New Testament. The same rebuttal work was carried on later by a group called the Church Fathers. Readers can Google names like Clement, Ignatius, Polycarp, Irenaeus and Tertullian if they are interested in going further into this issue.

By the early fourth century, recognised Church Councils felt obliged to issue official statements on the question of who Jesus was. Two stood out and became the most revered of all subsequent official creeds of Christendom. One is the Apostles' Creed which was concerned to spell out the humanity of Jesus. The other was the Nicene Creed which does its best to answer the doozy of a question how, if he were human, could he also be divine, and if he were divine, how could he be a human?

For better or worse, these two creeds became the standard norms and have proved to be the most serviceable, widely-used and durable since then. My own church's, red-covered, 674 page, *Uniting in Worship* order of service declares, 'These creeds are authoritative statements of faith and have a special place in worship'.[79] Also indicated is that traditionally the Nicene Creed is used when the Lord's Supper is celebrated, the Apostles' Creed for the rite of baptism. Allowance is also made for various ancient or modern statements of faith at other services and it is not unusual for this to occur. But the Apostle's Creed still ranks as the one most regularly used and also the one for best affirming what traditional Christianity believes about Jesus. G. K Chesterton (1874-1936), English author, philosopher and Christian apologist, one of the many champions for the Creed, wrote a book titled *Orthodoxy*. Here is one of his affirmations: 'the central Christian theology (sufficiently summarised in the Apostles' Creed) is the best root of energy and sound ethics'.[80]

Not all were so enamoured of this Creed or, if they once were, became less so. Phillip, whom we met in chapter two of this book, claimed to have got to his feet about 2,500 times in his church to recite the words of the Apostles' Creed as part of the various liturgies of the Anglican churches he attended in his sixty years of regular Sunday worship. We also noted that in the end he believed only five of the twenty or more of the affirmations. I suspect that large numbers of moderns who still attend their church are like this friend of mine. They stand to say the words of these creeds about Jesus, but they do not believe all of what they say. Some say the words because they are part of the overall liturgical furniture of historic Christianity. It is a way of affirming they are in this very special faith family. Others vocalise what they do not believe in order not to draw unwelcome attention to themselves.

This chapter now presents three brief segments about Jesus. First is a broad-brush profile of Jesus as presented by orthodox Christianity. Then comes some material from modern biblical scholarship which describes some of the big shifts in how to interpret the Gospels. The third is a profile of Jesus as presented by one representative of Progressive Christianity using these new tools.

First then a fairly standard profile of Jesus as presented by orthodox Christianity in its creeds, hymns, sermons, religious education programs, Sunday School syllabus liturgies, sacramental rites, Bible class materials and so on. For the record, there is no better place to find nearly all of these items than in the hymns so fondly and fervently sung by the faithful at Christmas and Easter. Very likely many of today's Baby Boomers were raised on this profile of Jesus.

It looks something like this:

- that Jesus had an eternal pre-existence before appearing on planet earth
- that he was conceived miraculously when the Holy Spirit of God fertilised the egg of a Palestinian virgin called Mary
- that as a consequence of this supernatural conception, he was endowed with the full attributes of God as well as those of a human being, each co-existing in equal proportions
- as a Palestinian Jew, Jesus progressively developed an awareness that he was the Messiah, the Saviour of the world
- he was endowed with miraculous abilities that he used to alleviate human suffering, and to point to a supernatural realm beyond this one, inhabited by one he called *Abba*: Father
- he specialised in teaching by parables that emphasised the ethics of love and justice
- his big theme was the Kingdom of God, a vision that gripped him.
- he anticipated the forming of organisations after his death and planted germinal seeds for their eventual governance structure
- he died on a Roman cross, but was miraculously brought back to life by his Father God
- his death was not only inevitable in human terms, but necessary in the divine order of things, that decreed one man had to die on behalf of all men and women

- after his resurrection, he made several Palestinian appearances to former acquaintances
- he left planet earth (observed by reliable witnesses) by ascending whence he came – the eternal dwelling place of God
- he re-established himself within the eternal Godhead, his primary task being to intercede with the Divine Father on behalf of humans, whom he himself once was
- these events, put together, enabled a release of the third person of the Trinity – the Holy Spirit – to earth in order to complete the salvation work of God
- he will triumphantly return to Earth in some future time to act as the final judge for those alive, as well as for those previously deceased.

An itemised list like this one summarising core orthodox doctrines about Jesus will be subject to various deletions, additions and general modifications, but conservative theology is likely to agree it is a reasonable summary of core beliefs about Jesus.

'Goodness gracious', a Bible study member blurted, 'There is not much left of Jesus if they want to get rid of all this!' when a similar list was presented as an example of conventional beliefs now under serious question. Defenders of orthodox Christianity are entirely with her. Take away these titles, powers, qualities, dimensions and achievements and Jesus, they assert, is reduced to nothing more than a standard humanist, just another in the pantheon of significant wise men or outstanding religious leaders.

Not so, progressive Christians reply. Releasing Jesus from the bondage of these creeds, titles and perspectives has much going for it. Take, for example, an inner-city clergy who has publicly described her Jesus as a *Palestinian Sage and a God-intoxicated prophet*. There is nothing anaemic about her Gospel, no diminution of her advocacy for this Jesus as a contemporary leader, a social activist, an advocate for inclusiveness, persistently on the side of the disadvantaged and disempowered. Note too that she points out how critical he was of official religion in his own times. Her Jesus is a spiritual, enabling presence, a sense of the Sacred a model of compassion and justice that is more than enough for her, and for most in her parish.[81]

It is difficult to assess how many there are like her. Even one of them is too many, according to her critics. There have always been people like her in Christendom, perhaps never more so than in past 150 years. During this time frame we have seen massive – yes, massive – shifts in mainline scholarship about Jesus and the Bible. Our way of understanding who Jesus was has been radically altered. We can call this a paradigm shift, a big picture way of changing our understanding.

Some of these big shifts that have affected the world of modern biblical scholarship include the following:

- science has replaced mythology. As author Arne Dahl has one of her characters say, 'myths and fantasies have always given way the moment science gains ground'[82]
- large sections of the Bible, once seen as historical narrative – photo shots, as it were of what took place, are now seen as saga, myth, poetry, legend, allegory
- vast numbers of the sayings of Jesus recorded in the four Gospels which were formerly accepted as coming from his lips are now seen as the beliefs of the early church. These editorial insertions were superimposed into the narrative as though they were his sayings and activities. They are statements of faith, not trustworthy biography
- the long-standing view of the Bible as a document that is divinely inspired, error- free and authoritative in matters of faith and morals has come under significant modification
- the science of literary criticism has made its presence felt in biblical interpretation. Texts are now interpreted in the context of their historical settings, the reasons for their composition, their various styles and major themes
- archaeological digs have discovered previously unknown papyrus texts which have shed fresh light on the world of Jesus' times, opening up new avenues of interpretation

- cross cultural studies on the Jewish/Roman world of Jesus' time have presented fresh ways of interpreting the message and behaviours of Jesus
- feminist studies have mounted a solid case for their belief that the read out of Jesus has been distorted by a post-Jesus masculine hierarchy.

In short, it all adds up to what Sportin' Life, Gershwin's character in *Porgy and Bess* claimed: 'the things that you're li'ble to read in the Bible, ain't necessarily so'.

As indicated, these big shifts have not been universally welcomed. Some have interpreted them as hostile attacks on God, on Christianity's Sacred Book and on religion at large. For others, however, these shifts have inspired greater respect for the Bible as literature; enriched the task of its interpretation; enhanced its reputation as one of the world's great sacred texts and radically changed views about how God engages with the universe and individuals. An exciting and liberating freedom has opened up to explore old territory in a fresh way with a good result.

So now to a progressive profile of Jesus, a collation of the views about Jesus which I have stitched together from the publications of Robert Funk, one of the contemporary revisionist biblical scholars. This is his take on Jesus.

- Jesus did exist
- he did not believe he was divine
- he was a party goer; that is, attended convivial gatherings sponsored by others
- he was a talker not a writer, belonging to an oral culture.
- he spoke with fresh authority
- he was possibly illiterate
- he spoke Aramaic and possibly Greek
- he didn't make theological statements like 'God is love' or 'Everyone is a sinner'
- he was not an eschatological prophet who expected that the world was about to end

- he did not make philosophical generalisations
- he refused to be explicit
- his preferred medium for delivering his message was parables
- he avoided practical advice
- his big theme was the kingdom of God
- he was none of the things the creeds say he was: born of the Virgin Mary, raised from the dead, ascended to God, part of a triune deity, set to come again to judge the world
- he did not see himself as a messiah
- he belonged to an oral culture
- he was not a sacrificial lamb who gave his life as a peace offering to God
- we do not know for a fact that he was buried
- he was a subversive sage (Funk's key idea about Jesus)
- he kept an open table
- he advocated an unbroken relationship with God
- he had nothing to say about himself, except that he had no address, no bed to sleep on and was not respected by his own
- he did not ask his disciples to establish a church
- he did not practise baptism.

Readers who have not gone into an apoplectic fit about this listing may wish to tick what appeals to them and why. Read Funk. Read the Gospels for yourself. See what you think. Read more on Funk and the way he went about reaching these views in chapter eleven. The two profiles about Jesus presented in this chapter – one orthodox and the other progressive – exist at the extreme opposite edges of Christianity. Perhaps they are best thought of as teasers or thought provokers for bold doubters.

Numerous other profiles or options exist between these two ends of the football field. Contemporary secular contributions are also available. For an intriguing example, try the 2010 novel *The Good Man Jesus and the Scoundrel Christ* by Philip Pullman. Mary has two boys. She calls one Jesus, the other Christ. They jostle with each other. They are different types. They have different agendas and personalities. Jesus is the modest, moral, spiritual one. The twin Christ is the scheming one who uses his brother's legacy, as one person put it, to found a powerful church. Meant as an allegory, some say, it is a provocative, highly fictionalised, controversial retelling of the Life of Jesus which in its own way attempts to portray the conflicting personalities superimposed upon the Galilean. It is worth a read. I enjoyed it. Richard Holloway, Bishop of Edinburgh during 1986-2000 gave it a positive review.

We now turn to the views of a cluster of biblical scholars who, over the last one hundred to one hundred and fifty years, sought to locate the original Jesus who they claim lies behind the Gospel narratives and the Creeds of Christendom. All of them were selected because they fulfilled my criterion that they demonstrate the rich diversity of views in biblical scholarship in modern times. Please don't sell biblical scholars short. They are an amazing collection of specialists absolutely devoted to making sense of the Sacred book of Christianity.

Chapter 9

Putting new clothes on Jesus

Albert Schweitzer's search for the historical Jesus

Albert Schweitzer is included here for multiple reasons. One of the most famous, if controversial, of Christian biblical scholars, he was passionate about releasing the spirit of Jesus from its imprisonment in the dogmas and official creeds of the church. He claimed that Jesus did not think dogmatically, did not formulate doctrine, and didn't judge anyone's belief 'by reference to any standard of doctrinal correctness'.[83] He did not believe that Jesus was resurrected from the dead, but that he comes to us as spirituality through his powerful sayings. Schweitzer was a critic of Christianity for not being 'full grown'; for doing much damage, and for failing to be what it could have been if Christianity had fully listened to the Jesus ethic of active love.

He also proposed that, although the ancient message of Jesus was necessarily presented in terms of the ideas and issues of his time, it must be *re-clothed* to address the issues of the modern world. Controversially, he asserted that neither Jesus nor the Bible promoted the idea that Jesus could do no wrong. Indeed, he believed that on one major issue Jesus got it dramatically wrong.

Schweitzer once wrote that all he wanted was to 'do something special in the spirit of Jesus'. Born in 1875, the son and grandson of Alsace Lutheran clergymen, he was to become world famous in three disciplines: music, theology and medicine. In music, he was an internationally recognised concert organist and an authority on his much-loved J. S. Bach. Not only did he write a famous biography of him in 1906, but five years later published a collaborative edition of his works for the organ with the equally famous organist and composer C. M Widor. In theology, he wrote several books on biblical topics, one of them, *The Quest for the Historical Jesus* (1906), destined to become both controversial and influential in Jesus studies. Thirdly, as though these careers were not sufficiently significant, he astounded his contemporaries by training as a medical doctor and sailing away from fame in Europe to practise as a medical missionary in the remote jungle at Lambarene, French Equatorial Africa. There he built and ran a hospital, which as we will see later, was to come under much criticism.[84]

Schweitzer belonged to the school of late nineteenth/early twentieth century scholars intent on recovering what they called the historical Jesus. He claimed that the Nicene Creed formulation of Jesus as both Man and God obliterated the historical man. Removing these 'grave clothes', as he called them, was necessary if the actual person were to be found. Few of the Quest for the Historical Jesus scholars saw any possibility of writing an accurate biography of Jesus. Only a handful of them concluded that Jesus never existed, or if he did, reduced him to an entirely secular figure. Of all the historical Jesus scholars, Schweitzer was the one most interested in rebutting the idea that Jesus was a psychologically disturbed, indeed paranoid individual, an assertion which was then being presented from some unsympathetic to Christianity. For his medical degree, Schweitzer presented his *The Psychiatric Study of Jesus*. In this work he concluded that the list of symptoms required to make a diagnosis of psychiatric illness could not be met in Jesus' case. 'He never behaves like a man wandering in a system of delusion', claimed Schweitzer.[85]

What did capture Schweitzer's interest, along with that of most of his fellow 'questers', was whether or not Jesus saw himself as the Messiah. This was the sixty-four-thousand-dollar question of the day. Using the new critical tools of that time, Schweitzer's reading of the Gospels led him to the view that it would have been impossible for Jesus not to have had such a question in his own mind. Not only would he have wondered if he might be that figure, so too might his mother. In many a Jewish pregnant mother's heart existed a burning hope, both then and before, that her boy might be that Coming One. Biblical scholars of Schweitzer's times claimed that 30 A.D. in Palestine was alive with a heightened religious atmosphere created by a full-blown expectation of the imminent arrival of the long-promised Messiah. They referred to this as the late Judaist belief of Jesus' times. God was about to come to earth and establish an everlasting kingdom. One order was coming to its end. Another would be ushered in. The End Time drama was upon them. A supernatural Kingdom was about to arrive and transform everything. The Son of Man – the decisive apocalyptic figure of Judaism – was about to show himself.

Schweitzer's studies led him to conclude that Jesus did come to the view of himself as the Messiah. But he never said so to anyone. He kept it a secret. He also believed that this dramatic end of time event would occur in his lifetime and that he would be declared the longed-for Son of Man. He also accepted the commonly-held view of his times that the authentic Messiah would not 'step out of concealment' until the Messianic Kingdom arrived.[86]

But now comes a novel twist. According to Schweitzer, Jesus also accepted, as did many of his time, that before the Son of Man appeared there must first be a tribulation, a period of great suffering characterised by many signs and wonders. When this was not forthcoming – according to Schweitzer's reading of the material – Jesus decided to hasten or short-circuit the process. He would bargain with God to abolish the terrible period of calamity and suffering. He would offer himself to God as an atoning figure. This, he believed, would serve as a substitute for the foreseeable agonies that were necessary for the arrival of God's Kingdom. He would, as it were, force God's hand to hurry up the schedule. Schweitzer writes that Jesus was aware that a suffering servant of God would bear the guilt of others as prophesied in the book of Isaiah. Jesus resolved secretly to bear that guilt. He decided to precipitate his arrest and bring on his death.

If readers are not familiar with this big idea of a coming Kingdom so prevalent in Jesus' times, a quick Google search under Jewish Eschatology will be enlightening. The Christianising of this issue is found in the gospels. Mark 13 and Matthew 24 for example, provide vivid descriptions of what will happen when the Kingdom appears on earth. Best not to read some of this just before bedtime unless you are seeking a vivid, nightmarish horror show depicting how the end times will play out. Buildings will collapse; nations will engage in terrible wars; there will be earthquakes and famines a-plenty. Jesus calls these 'the birth pangs of the new age' (Mark 13:8). People will turn against each other. Fathers will betray their children. Children will turn violently against their parents, even to the point of killing them. Brother will betray brother.

And believe it or not, Jesus is even reported to have said that you wouldn't want to be a pregnant woman or have a child at the breast in a time like this. Not great news presumably for his own sisters, or extended family, or the women of his village or any women anywhere for that matter who were listening to him. As for Jesus' own disciples, he warns them they would be handed over to the courts to be flogged in their local synagogue. It was judgment time. The Son of Man would separate the sheep from the goats. The goats (unbelievers and those who did no good works) would be sent to eternal punishment. The sheep (the believers who did good works in God's name) were to be granted eternal life (Matthew 25:31-46).

Mark's version of this event has Jesus declaring that these things would happen in the foreseeable future, in fact very soon. Indeed, he is quoted as having said, 'Verily I say to you, that this generation shall not pass, till all these things be done' (Mark 13:30). In this expectancy, wrote Schweitzer, Jesus was wrong. The grand new Kingdom did not eventuate, neither with nor without a horrible time of tribulation. Enormous relief, no doubt, to the pregnant women or new mothers he had referred to. As for Jesus, he did not come back to life. He wasn't declared and celebrated as the Messiah. His destiny was not to preside over the end times of everything.

Schweitzer acknowledged that many would be shocked at the idea that Jesus was capable of error in believing that 'what he announced as imminent, did not appear'.[87] But, he observes, Jesus never made any claim to omniscience. The 'Christ personality of dogma' may have presented him as 'omniscient and incapable of error', but he did not see himself that way. Indeed, when a young man addressed him as Good Master,[88] he pointed out that God alone is good. Those who came after him may have attributed divinity to him, but he never claimed it nor saw himself to be so.

Getting it badly wrong did not diminish Jesus in Schweitzer's estimation. The power of his sayings on humanity were far more crucial than his failure to get it right about the end times. What impressed Schweitzer about Jesus was his 'personality as it is'.[89] This influences us much more strongly and immediately than the Jesus who comes to us in dogma, he claims. All we need to do is to look at 'the historical Jesus straight in the face and listen for what He may have to teach in his powerful sayings'.[90] The true relation with Jesus is to be found only in being possessed by him. This happens when we allow his powerful sayings to exert their influence on us. They can do that. Jesus lives on in them.

What is so special about these sayings is that they are all about active love, a life-promoting precept in the context of a life-negating one. Love is the supreme ethical requirement in all things, including even in an end-of-the-world scenario. Schweitzer's religious philosophy is not about opening ourselves to an unconditional divine love that forgives us our sins. Joining God in the active ethic of love is the invitation of the Jesus. If and when we encounter this God, what we will discover and experience is the will to love. We will be caught up in and influenced by what God is: an active spiritual force, 'a beam of which reaches us from the infinite'.[91] A powerful 'ethical energy 'drives us. This God challenges us with an imperative: to love.[92] Schweitzer uses the word pantheistic about this experience, but only in the sense that everything that exists has its being in the first Great Cause of all being. Living Christianity is not a 'nature religion'. It can't be, because it is about relating to an ethical personality at whose heart is the Will-to Live and Will-to Love.

By now, we have arrived at another somewhat startling theme of Schweitzer's view of Christianity. His Jesus is not presenting himself as an object of religious faith. We are not to believe in him. Schweitzer's Jesus is no good for a Sunday night altar call to come to Jesus and be saved. His Jesus wants us to look away from himself to what he was pointing towards: union with God in the activity of love.

Schweitzer had a lover's quarrel with historic Christianity. For a period of his life, he studied the world religions in order to see which were what he characterised as *world- and life-affirming* and those which were *world- and life-negating*. Christianity and Hinduism emerged well compared with some of the other religions but each, he claimed, contained too much life-negating. He saw the very early Christian church as life-denying because it clung to a belief in the imminent end of the world and showed no interest in improving the human condition. But at the same time, there was a life-affirming content in early Christianity because it also contained concurrently the active ethic of Jesus. Schweitzer also recognised certain modern epochs under the sway of the life-affirming ethos because they were able to lay aside the primitive church expectation of the end of the world.[93]

When Schweitzer's ethic of love is *widened into universality*, it becomes Reverence for Life, the phrase with which his name is so famously attached, first introduced publicly as a sermon title on 16 February 1919 at Strasburg. Reverence for life was more than a belief. It was a practice he sustained until his death. Thus, he actively opposed the ill-treatment of animals in popular amusements. He decided to do good in neglected parts of Africa, where he built his hospital, often returning to Europe to give benefit concerts in order to raise funds. He presented learned articles on the basic human rights: to shelter and housing; to education, and to protection under the law. He joined the Ban the Bomb movement and protested against the use of torture in war and peacetime, an involvement that earned him the Nobel Peace Prize.

Schweitzer died on 4 September 1965 and was buried at Lambourne, as also was his wife. His time and fame were to fade, as did Mother Theresa's in India. His Lambourne medical project was to undergo major criticisms, hers likewise. He was deemed to be paternalistic, his methods condescending and racist. He was also criticised for maintaining sub-standard wards in his hospital which he defended on the grounds that his patients were more likely to stay for treatment in keeping with their jungle homes than they would have in modern medical facilities.

Biblical scholarship that came after Schweitzer also moved on, claiming that Jesus did not believe in an imminent new order of things or its opposite, an end time for everything. The biblical texts that seemed to support that view were now deemed by scholars not to belong to Jesus.

But much of what Schweitzer wrote continues to have enormous appeal. His view of God as will-to-live and will-to-love is robust, life-affirming and life-equipping. The humanising of Jesus is also appealing to many, as well as the active ethic of love. How tantalising is his view that the *curious history* of the study of the life of Jesus only reinforces the view that 'The historical Jesus will be to our time a stranger and an enigma'.[94] He wrote that in 1910, but surely, he knew that he was writing for all times. As the last paragraph of his famous work put it: 'He comes to us as One unknown, without a name, as of old by the lake-side, he came to those who knew him not. He speaks to us the same word: 'Follow me!' and sets us to the tasks which he has to fulfil for our time'.[95]

Schweitzer's view was that each generation or epoch must find its own thoughts about Jesus. It is the only way they can make him live. To use his metaphor, the clothes in which the active love message of Jesus is presented may fit one epoch but not another. Re-clothing Jesus is always called for. A cluster of other German biblical scholars did just that. To just one of them we now turn. He does not use the image of clothing. His chosen image is that of the common onion.

Chapter 10

The onion man of biblical interpretation

Rudolph Bultmann and de-mythologising

Picture your minister walking into the pulpit one Sunday morning, holding aloft an onion and proceeding to preach a sermon about it. This chapter is about the man who used that image in his effort to present Jesus and Christianity stripped of mythical pre-scientific views of the world. Whether he succeeded or not depends on your point of view, but in times like these, he probably gets some brownie points for having a go. His name is Rudolph Bultmann (1884-1976). This chapter gives a brief summary of his big themes which are *de-mythologise, be what you are*, and *kerygma*.

Like Schweitzer, his father and grandfather were clergy, his father a German Lutheran pastor, his grandfather a missionary in West Africa. He was never in doubt about his career path. He wanted only to be an academic theologian. At age nineteen, he began his theological studies at the University of Tubingen. In 1921, he became Professor of New Testament at the University of Marburg and remained in that position until his retirement in 1951. He is now recognised as one of the most influential scholars and theologians of the early 20th century. He was also one of the several Protestant theologians who spoke out publicly against the rise to power of Adolf Hitler.

Bultmann's scholarly mission was to disassociate Jesus from the mythological world view of New Testament. If we fail to do that, he predicted, the fallout for Christianity will be calamitous. It is both 'senseless and impossible', he declared,[96] to expect modern minds to accept mythical, pre-scientific views of the world as part and parcel of Christian teaching. He proposed an alternative: release the Jesus story from the primitive mythological world view of the time.

This brings us to his onion image. Bultmann acknowledges that an onion is not a perfect image because onions do not have a core. Nevertheless, he uses it to illustrate his theme that the essential, inner message of Jesus can be discovered only by stripping from the biblical narratives the pre-scientific, mythological beliefs of Jesus' times in which his story is set. He described that process as de-mythologising.

I remember reading Bultmann's ninety-eight-page paperback *Jesus Christ and Mythology* on this topic while at university in 1959. I still have it. I was not overly impressed, but my copious marginal notes indicate that I had been somehow stirred up. The onion image resurfaced a few decades later as I, like many of that time, began to discard beliefs which I had previously considered to be quintessential to Christian belief. But if his process of shedding the mythological elements helped validate what I was doing, his alternative, unfortunately, was not helpful, as we will see.

Bultmann didn't invent the de-mythologising word, but he did normalise its use in New Testament studies. Your dictionary will tell you it means to set free or divest a piece of literature of its mythical elements. What then are these pre-scientific, mythological, outer onion leaves which he believed required peeling? The idea of a God living above us in a local heaven is a good example. It may well be, he wrote, a romantic view, but certainly not a believable one. Nor was the idea of a hell located somewhere deep below us, beneath our feet, to which – according to the Apostles' Creed – Jesus descended, and from which he ascended into heaven. Equally mythological is the biblical view that various disorders of the mind and body – epilepsy, migraines, blindness, paralysis, blood disorders, to name a few – are the work of the Devil and his zillions of demons. The idea that humans died because one man – Adam – was disobedient to God, he described as 'sheer nonsense'. Similarly, the idea of original sin as an inherited infection is 'sub-ethical, irrational, and absurd'.[97] The same objection applies to the idea that the guilt of one man can be expiated by the death of a sinless other.

There is more. 'The idea that a divine Being should become incarnate and atone for the sins of men through his own blood' is 'irrational and meaningless'. Also categorised as myth is the notion of the pre-existence of Jesus. Bultmann is prepared to accept that there was a Palestinian Jew of that name, 'about whom the Sacred book of Christianity writes', but '... it is questionable whether Jesus regarded himself as Messiah at all'.[98]

In short, the New Testament world view is no longer convincing to the modern mind. Science and technology have provided credible explanations for what a long time ago required supernatural ones. We have discovered the forces and laws of nature. We can no longer believe in, nor need, spirits, good or evil. Bultmann's position is encapsulated in this oft-quoted statement: 'It is impossible to use electric light and the wireless and to avail ourselves of modern medical and surgical discoveries, and at the same time believe in the New Testament world of spirits and miracles'.[99]

Surprisingly, perhaps, Bultmann now asks us to be respectful of all this mythology. Myth ought not to be laughed at, dismissed, disbelieved. Rather myth ought to be interpreted. Myths, he proposes, may be a primitive science, but they carry enduring truths and deep meanings. The task for the modern reader is to search for these truths. He describes this process as stripping 'the mythological framework from the truth they enshrine'.[100] Seek the point inherent in the imagery.

Take for example the Bible writer's primitive construction of the universe as a vast three-storey construction. The top storey – heaven – was seen as God's domicile. Search for the deeper meaning inside the outer wrapping, and we find, claims Bultmann, the idea that God is beyond the world. The core idea is that of transcendence. The middle storey is earth, where humans dwell. The bottom story – the one furthest from God – is Hell, the dwelling place of Satan and his vast cohort. De-mythologise Hell and it becomes evil as 'a tremendous power which again and again afflicts mankind'.[101]

How then does Bultmann go about his task of de-mythologising Jesus? There are so many mythological outer leaves about Jesus which he wants to strip away: the virgin birth, the pre-existence of Jesus, his divinity, that he was the Messiah and knew it, his capacity to perform miracles, his sacrificial death, his descent into hell, his resurrection and his ascension back to heaven.

What does remain for Bultmann's Jesus as an historical figure is that he was a prophet and a rabbi. He was not a Christian and he never according to Bultmann summoned others 'to acknowledge' or 'believe in' his person.[102] As prophet he 'proclaims the irruption of God's reign'.[103] His message is that the kingdom of God is coming and all must prepare themselves for it. The reign of God is breaking. Be open to it. Jesus is a protester standing in the line of the ancient Jewish prophets who promoted radical obedience to God rather than rituals and the religious law.

As a prophet of God, Bultmann claims, Jesus shared the conviction of his era, of a soon-to-come, fearful, eschatological drama. Bultmann writes 'Jesus envisaged the inauguration of the Kingdom as a tremendous cosmic drama'.[104] Out from the clouds of heaven, the Son of Man would descend. Those already dead would be raised to join the living. The righteous would face bliss. The damned would be delivered to the torments of hell. This kingdom would come in the near future and all must be prepared to face God's judgment.

But Bultmann claims that if Jesus did share this Jewish hope and expectation, he did not see himself as the Son of Man, as the Messiah. His task was to point to that man. And, writes Bultmann, in his thinking that the End is destined to come, 'he was mistaken'.[105] Or, as he puts it elsewhere, 'Jesus' expectation of the near end of the world turned out to be an illusion'.[106] But Jesus was not on his own about this imminent cosmic drama, reports Bultmann, other Jewish prophets had also been wrong.

Before discussing Bultmann's next step, it is worth explaining how he reached his conclusions about who Jesus was and what he did. Modern Bultmann type biblical scholars do not just peel away from the biblical story about Jesus what they don't like about that story. There is science to their method, as explained in chapter eight. Using the tools of literary criticism and historical research, they reached the conclusion that some of what is put into the mouth of Jesus in the Gospels is not likely to have been spoken by him. This claim is, of course, unacceptable to conservative biblical scholars. They argue that the four Gospels are an accurate record of what Jesus did and said. They may have been written by individuals, but they were also inspired (God breathed) and are therefore infallible (free of error.) What they report as happening did happen in time and place.

Bultmann type scholars see the Gospel narratives differently. What we have in Matthew, Mark, Luke and John is a retelling of the Jesus story from the point of view of the early Christian communities which sprang up after his death. After his death, his story was spread by word of mouth, transmitted both by those who knew him and those who did not. Decades later, they were set down in writing. During both periods (the oral and the written), the stories about what he said and what he did were modified to fit the needs, circumstances and ceremonies of those new faith communities such as baptism and other initiation rites, faith formation, dealing with persecution, how to be a Jesus disciple, etc. Eventually, the teaching officials of the growing church selected what, in their view, were the best and the most useful ones in telling the Jesus story and guiding the new religion. This was the accreditation phase. These stories were gathered into the collection we now call the New Testament. The first of these Gospels (Mark) was in its final form around thirty years after the death of Jesus and the last one (John) up to seventy or eighty years after Jesus' death.

In order to separate what was original to Jesus and what was the early church faith story about him, Bultmann employed a scholarly tool which he invented called Form Criticism. As the name implies, this involved a study of the literary forms used in the Gospels. They included miracle stories, proverbs, what he called apothegms (sayings associated with an event or a scene), parables, historical narratives and apocalyptic sayings. About this process he wrote: 'The purpose of Form Criticism is to study the history of the oral tradition behind the Gospels'.[107]

Using this and other tools, Bultmann reached his conclusion that there was a vast difference between (i) Jesus stripped of myth – the historical Jesus – and (ii) the Jesus presented in the Gospels – the Jesus of faith. Peel away the mythical overlay of Jesus identity and what remains is, as we have indicated, a Jewish prophet with a message about the imminent arrival of God's Kingdom together with a summons to be ready. God is about to act is the central Jesus message. Be ready for it. This is Jesus the proclaimer. Searching for any further historical detail, Bultmann claims, is fruitless.

So where did Bultmann go next? Since his Jesus picture fits into his much bigger God picture, a few explanations about that are appropriate. Bultmann is nothing if not a classic case of an unapologetic theist. He feels no need to find proofs for God whom he sees as a given in his biblical theology discipline. His deity is certainly a God botherer in that phrase's original usage of a deity always bothering humans about something, not a human always bothering others about God. His writing is full of God language. God is transcendent. God is the 'unseen beyond'. God is the Creator of the world. God is also the 'One who comes'. God speaks. God acts. God speaks to humans in the here and now. God addresses each hearer as a self. And God is always benevolent, constantly ahead of us, 'being where we would like to be'.

Bultmann also stresses the classical religious theme that authentic human security can be found 'only in the unseen beyond in God'. Humans need to abandon mere human security. Life is fleeting and its end is death. Real security cannot be found by organising our personal and community life. If humans forget the beyond they cannot find freedom from the world and from sorrow and anxiety. Only when 'the Word of God addresses man in his personal existence' can that freedom be found.[108]

This brings us to Bultmann's second big theme. First was *demythologise*. Now we come to *be what you are*. He claims this is the teaching of the New Testament. 'Man has to undertake to be what he already is.'[109] This is what Bultmann's God calls humans to be and to make a choice about. At this point, Bultmann is incorporating into his theistic presentation a big idea from a fellow professor of his at Marburg, to whom he became a good friend, Martin Heidegger, one of the foremost advocates of existentialism, a popular philosophical movement of his time.[110] Existentialism explores the miseries, the grandeur, the contradictions of human existence. Angst, dread and entrapment are its big themes, but equally strong are the themes of freedom and choice. Here was a perfect vehicle for Bultmann to use in explaining and promoting his theistic vision of a God who calls humans to decision-making.

Bultmann found in existentialism the concept of authenticity. He writes with approval, even excitement, about the phrase *be what you are*. Bultmann is of the view that God works only with things as they are. God does not make anything into something it is not. To be more of what they naturally are is God's desire for humans. To fail to be that sort of person leads to what he calls the *inauthentic life*. And this he writes is what the Bible means by sin.

Existential literature also gave Bultmann another explanation for why humans fall short of being what they are intended to be. Anxiety is the culprit. Anxiety stops humans from achieving authenticity. He quotes with approval Paul's view that humans are *weighed down* (1 Corinthians 7:32ff) or *become a slave* (Romans 8:15) to this debilitating state of mind. We bring this enslavement on ourselves, he argues, by choosing false or worldly securities. The authentic life needs to be grounded in 'intangible realities'.[111] Chief of these is the forgiveness of God, for it is this grace of God that 'releases us from the past' and opens us 'freely to the future'.[112]

Back now to Jesus and to Bultmann's third big theme *kerygma*. *Kerygma* is an ancient Greek word meaning a *proclamation*. The *kerygma*, according to Bultmann, is the material about Jesus found in the Gospels and Paul which is presented from the point of view of faith. It is what the believing community affirmed about him. And this belief, writes Bultmann, is based on their experience of him. He may have died, but he was a living presence for them. He was alive and real for them. Their Jesus was resurrected.

Bultmann writes that the Resurrection narratives were composed 'in the interests of faith and under the influence of devout imagination'.[113] Theologian Alistair McGrath, as with many others, when trying to interpret Bultmann at this point, writes that Bultmann's view of the resurrection is that it is 'something which happened in the subjective experience of the disciples, not something which took place in the public arena of history'.[114] And as befits a resurrected figure, they endow him with various titles and abilities and name him 'the Crucified and Risen One'. A dramatic switch has occurred. *The proclaimer became the proclaimed*, is how Bultmann describes this transformation of Jesus.

Christianity commences at this point with the community after him seeing and experiencing him as someone he did not see himself to be. A Palestinian, Jewish prophet with a message about someone else has become the central point of a new message which will now go by the name of Christianity. And this faith story of the early Jesus followers is the core message that God uses and is the one to be preached today. Pay attention to this *kerygma* he insists. This is where God speaks and confronts.

Bultmann's writing is full of these kinds of efforts to take up classical Christian ideas and subject them to his de-mythologising process. God in heaven has become the transcendent One who calls us to decision-making, not about some future cosmic event, but about our own selfhood. Jesus did not come back from the dead in any historical or bodily sense but he still lives on in the *kerygma* of the church and can be experienced as a here-and-now presence. Sin is not doing bad stuff and showing defiance to God. Sin is falling short of our own humanity.

His demythologising of the Cross may also appeal to some. He links the crucifixion of Jesus with the resurrection. The Cross was a cruel event but Jesus was not crucified 'for us' as a sacrifice to pay for the sins of the world. He sees the Cross as having what he calls redemptive significance when we 'make the Cross our own, by undergoing crucifixion with Jesus'.[115] He explains that to mean that we are invited to crucify our 'affections and lusts, overcome our dread of suffering', and develop detachments from what he calls *the world*. And if the resurrection is a lived experience with Jesus (not a historical event), Christians can also participate in the resurrection experience when 'they enjoy a freedom, albeit a struggling freedom, from sin'.[116]

There is no doubt that many will wave goodbye to Bultmann at this point. Having rejected the resurrection of Jesus as non-historical and mythical, he has now contrived to make it central to his version of the legitimate Christian message. No, thank you, they will say. Just another example of a religion constructing fanciful stories about their hero's birth and/or return from the dead. As for the orthodox, they won't have a bar of the idea that Jesus resurrection is anything else but historical fact. No resurrection, no Christianity, is their mantra. The moderates are a mixed bag, some loath to deny the historicity of the resurrection but others more likely to find ways of emphasising the rising as a symbol of new life. They are the ones more likely to speak about eggs on Easter morning. The progressives flat out deny he came back from the dead. Like Schweitzer, they do not need Jesus to be a historically resurrected figure to legitimise his mighty impact on religious experience and humanity at large.

Some readers may find themselves attracted to this brief portraiture of Bultmann's religious viewpoint. They may wish to take that interest further. Then there are those who may feel they have been led down the garden path. A promising start led to an unsatisfactory destination. Stripping away the mythical picture of Jesus was full of promise, but they reject Bultmann's alternative.

However, all may not be lost or wasted. At the very least, the onion image legitimatises the abandoning of the religion of their childhood and sets them free to search for an alternative to the one Bultmann proposes. And this is what many have done or are doing. They are open to the possibility, one that Bultmann disallows, of re-representing Jesus as a social revolutionary, or a humanitarian activist, or a healer, or an ethical teacher, or feminine Wisdom figure, or peace maker, or Good Samaritan, or sage or God's Man for others, or spiritual mentor.

To that possibility we now turn. What follows are the views of five very modern post-scholars – two male, three female – who went searching for a different way, as Schweitzer put it, of putting fresh clothes on Jesus.

Chapter 11

Jesus as Subversive Sage

The Jesus Movement of Robert Funk and others

The Jesus Seminar 1: Robert Funk

One of the more radical Jesus revisionists of recent times was Robert W. Funk. Like Schweitzer and Bultmann, he was motivated by the belief that behind the Jesus of the Gospels and the creeds of Christendom lurks an unknown Jesus. What he claims to discover is Jesus the *subversive sage*. Inadequate and wrong, according to orthodoxy. Full of possibility, based on responsible and accurate scholarship, claim others.

In the same way as others on the lookout for an alternative from the received teachings of their youth, Funk was searching for a different Jesus. He writes that he began his Christianity quite young with a 'string of beliefs and very little faith',[117] and was strongly convinced that it was important to hold 'correct opinions'. His high school grades won him a scholarship to study law at Indiana University, but his local minister persuaded him that he would make a good clergyman. He commenced a program in an eastern Tennessee Bible College, the 'simplistic creed' of which displeased him.

After two years, Funk transferred to Butler University in Indianapolis. There he found that the training for parish ministry also displeased him. He felt that a search for truth was not compatible with the role of a clergy person. He became a scholar, but in order to 'stay near the church' taught in theological seminaries for the next twenty years, after which he concluded that 'the old theological issues had become limp and lifeless'. Transferring to a secular university, he encountered the very thing from which he was attempting to escape. Universities and churches, he decided, can each be alike in their 'orthodoxies of various kinds, their courts of inquisitions, and penalties for those who seek intellectual freedom'.

He went solo, retired, founded a publishing house and set up what he called the Westar Institute, dedicated to private research. Funk decided to invite thirty fellow biblical scholars to join with him in the task of collecting and analysing the words and deeds of Jesus as used in ancient sources up to 300 AD. He believed that no-one had ever done this before and certainly not on such a grand scale. They would examine approximately 1,500 versions of the 500 sayings attributed to Jesus in the four Gospels and other texts of that time. These included a document called Q and a Gospel named Thomas, now well-known to biblical scholars of modern times.

Each of the thirty was asked to invite others, which they did, and as a result around 120 -150 scholars joined in the project. They gave themselves the name The Jesus Seminar, and met for six years before going public with their findings. All the scholars had been involved in Gospel research before joining this program and came largely from mainline denominations. Fundamentalist scholars were invited, but declined to participate.

At the opening meeting of the Seminar, Funk said about Jesus: 'We are in quest of his *voice*, insofar as it can be distinguished from many other voices also preserved in the tradition'.[118] Funk correctly asserted that distinguishing the 'authentic speech' of Jesus from what he called 'the interpretive overlay' of the four gospels was a 'well established procedure' among gospel scholars, one that had been operative for over two hundred years of biblical scholarship'.[119]

Teams of up to forty scholars gathered twice yearly to discuss previously circulated material on different sets of Jesus sayings (the parables, the Sermon on the Mount, the kingdom of God) debating them one by one. When the scholars had completed what they wished to contribute to the debate, a secret ballot was held, using a method in which each Fellow put a coloured bead into the ballot box.

Four colours – red, pink, grey and black – indicated a decision on the authenticity of each saying. Red: Jesus said it or it was very close; pink: he probably spoke of something like it; grey: they were not his but ideas but close to his; black: he did not say them, they were viewpoints of the Christian community that emerged after his death.

When Jesus' actions (rather than words) were under consideration, red accepted the reports as historically reliable; pink, probably reliable; grey, possible but lacking supporting evidence; and black, improbable, cannot be verified or may even be fictitious.

On the key issue of the authenticity of Jesus utterances, Funk wrote that 'on a case by case basis, less than 20 percent of the words attributed to Jesus in the Gospels was actually spoken by him'.[120] That claim certainly set the cat among the pigeons. He also adds that it was a miracle that so many survived at all.

The next step was to integrate the authenticated sayings with the authenticated deeds of Jesus on which the Seminar had also been working. Having completed this 'twin database',[121] they moved on to construct a profile of the historical Jesus and to compare it with past presentations of Jesus. Funk claimed that there was nothing unusual in Christianity about the use of this methodology.

What picture of Jesus emerged for Funk from the Seminar? I have already profiled that in dot form in chapter eight. Time now to enlarge on that profile. Funk's key description of Jesus was that he was a *subversive sage*. *Subversive* points to him as a Jewish religious person and a citizen of the Roman Empire who overturned the way things were done in his culture. *Sage* refers to him as a person of venerated wisdom, as demonstrated in his famous sayings (his parables, aphorisms and proverbs).

Funk points out that Jesus was not the only sage of history, but was definitely one of the great ones. Noteworthy too, for Funk, was that Jesus as sage was *impious, irreligious* and *irreverent*. He profaned the temple, the Sabbath and the purity of his own times and spoke about the kingdom of God non-religiously. Like other sages of his times, he would have performed miracles, usually involving psychosomatic states.

Funk pays close attention to the conviviality of Jesus, describing him as what today might be designated an *urban partygoer*. He enjoyed an open table at which there were lively conversations over good food and drink. While lacking the means to sponsor gatherings or symposia, as they were then called, he did not hesitate to attend when these were sponsored by others. The accusation made against him by his critics that he was *a glutton and drunk* was not, according to Funk, to be taken literally. It was a recognised epithet of his times for sons who were incorrigible, or *deemed to be disobedient*.

To the charge that Jesus associated with *sinners*, Funk points out that these were judged to be outsiders in Jesus society: lepers, the maimed, the blind, gentiles, Samaritans, tax officials and women who did not observe the appropriate social mores. When charged by Pharisees for fraternising with such people, Jesus retorted that tax collectors and prostitutes would be welcomed into the kingdom but *you will not*.

Funk prefers the word *domain* for the biblical word kingdom, a word so central to the Gospel stories. Welcome in the domain of God are sinners and outcasts: Jew, gentile, slave, free, male and female. Those who think they are in may miss out. Social roles will be reversed. The marginal are in. The respectable may not be.

Funk claims that the key thing about Jesus is that he promoted *an unbrokered relationship with God*. He insisted that everyone has *immediate and particular access to God*. Accordingly, *priests and their temples are obsolete*. He finds no evidence that Jesus trained his disciples to 'convert the world', and establish an institution called the church. Nor did he make himself *the proper object of faith*. Others after him did that by naming him Lord and Saviour. Funk coins a phrase about this: *the iconoclast became the icon*.[122] They turned him into a divine salvation figure who invites faith in himself. The prophetic mission of Jesus was to *trust the Father, believe in God's domain or reign*.

Negative, even hostile, reactions to Funk (and the Jesus Seminar) were foreseeable and inevitable. Here are five of them. One is that the images and profile of Jesus presented by the Seminar, and especially by Funk, are incompatible with the mainstream teachings of historic Christianity. Denuding Jesus of his divinity and Saviourhood is contrary to the biblical message and the Creeds. It is heresy. Secondly, the Seminar was a self-created, independent agency, existing outside any of the formal denominational church bodies and therefore had no legitimate claim to the authority to speak for organised Christianity. Thirdly, Funk and the Seminar gave more prominence to the Gospel of Thomas than was allowable. That writing had not been included in the list of 66 books declared by the Council of Hippo in AD 393 to be inspired by God and worthy of inclusion in the Sacred Scriptures of Christianity. Matthew, Mark, Luke and John made it. Thomas didn't.

Criticism of The Seminar's voting procedure was also inevitable. Marcus Borg, a prominent participant, whom we discuss in a few pages, objected that historical questions cannot be determined by voting. Majority decisions can get things wrong. But he defends the Seminar's use of the method by asserting that voting such as this does measure current scholarly opinion. It discloses an existing consensus within a certain group of scholars. Presumably we could also add that this procedure is similar to the one used by the venerable Fathers who settled on the Canon back there 1700 years ago and likewise when the creeds of Christendom were formalised, not to mention the current practice in many church councils to measure consensus by coloured cards held high rather than voice volume.

A fifth and substantial criticism concerned the criteria used to determine what was authentic and what wasn't.[123] The Seminar members took pains in their literature to explain how they went about this process. The footnote explains the four *rules of evidence*, as they called them, in determining what was the voice of Jesus and what was the voice of the early church. No doubt they had in mind the inevitable criticism that they were modernists engaged in dumping what they didn't like and keeping only what suited them. Reminiscent, perhaps, of Thomas Jefferson, President of the USA who, according to John Meacham, had a crack at creating his own version of the Gospels. He did this by excising 'the New Testament passages he found supernatural or implausible, and then arranging the remaining verses in the order he believed they should be read'.[124]

Funk had no qualms about confronting orthodox critics of the Seminar's methods. He claimed there were big reasons for their refusal to accept the results of modern biblical scholarship, whether his or any anyone else's. They were trapped by a view that the Bible had divine authorship: the doctrine of inspiration. As a consequence, no errors were possible about what it taught. This was their doctrine of the Bible's infallibility. They also had a commitment to interpreting the Bible literally. For good value, he also accused them of patronage, ignorance, elitism and secret keeping.[125]

Funk was not on a mission to destroy Christianity or the organised church. He believed Christianity was a tradition that was worthy reforming and saving and that had often shown its power to reconstitute itself. Funk notes that liberating Jesus from mythological and supernatural understandings of him could contribute to that re-emergence.

Whatever the foibles, follies and fallacies of Funk's contribution to biblical scholarship, in both his own publications and those of his fellow scholars, the work and publications of the Jesus Seminar have, in the judgment of some scholars, cast a valuable pebble into the pool of Jesus studies. If you are after a radical de-mystifying of Jesus for the modern world, this one is worth a good look at. Numerous books, conferences and debates have sprung from the Jesus Seminar, spreading the claims of the movement. Two-day conferences were conducted in North America, New Zealand and the United Kingdom and Funk himself led a July 2000 three-lecture program at St Michael's Church, Melbourne. Two seminars followed The Jesus Seminar: *God and the Human Future* and *The Christianity Seminar*.

Funk died in September 2005. He was in the middle of writing a book on *The Incredible Christ* as well as a Seminar program on a new translation of Paul's letters when he was diagnosed with an aggressive brain tumour. He was to live only four months more. The Jesus Seminar dissolved one year later.

The Jesus Seminar II: Marcus Borg

If Funk can be seen as the leader of the trumpet section of the Jesus Seminar orchestra, Robert Borg (1942-2021) is certainly the leader of its cello section. He is widely recognised as a New Testament biblical scholar, the author of twenty-one books and was often seen and heard on the lecture circuit. One colleague noted that he travelled so often he accumulated 100,000 frequent flier miles annually. He was well established as a scholar before the Jesus Seminar and, like many of that movement's adherents, continued to incorporate the results of that program into the future directions of his own scholarship.

Born of Lutheran parents in Minnesota, USA, Borg undertook his post graduate religious studies at Oxford, UK. He spent most of his academic life in State Universities in America before retiring as Professor of Religion and Culture at Oregon State University in 2007. He was recognised as a major liberal scholar in Jesus studies and appeared on national TV debating various religious issues.

His strong interest in cross-cultural studies on the period in which Jesus lived led him to highlight the degree to which Jesus broke with attitudes to women in his times. A strong advocate for isolating the Jesus voice from that of his followers, Borg nevertheless favours using both voices in presenting Christianity. To strip the Jesus voice of its early church overlay, Borg claims, is to find a Jewish mystic with five profiles: spirit person, healer, wisdom teacher, social prophet and movement initiator.

Borg was well aware that the results of the Seminar enquiry could be perceived both within and outside the churches as 'anti-Christian and anti-church', in terms of its 'intention and results or both'.[126] He asserts it was not intended that way, nor need it be seen as a threat to the historical basis of Christianity. He asserts that the quest for *the voice of Jesus* – the purpose of the Seminar search – can be an ally within the church as it seeks a 'clearer understanding of Jesus, the gospels, Christian origins and (more broadly) the Bible itself'.[127] He also makes the point that different results from those of a Jesus Seminar held in 10 or 20-years' time would be likely.

Borg noted that some of the majority results were surprising, even sensational. For example, that Jesus did not think of himself as Messiah or the 'son of God', and did not see his own death as the purpose of his life. Unexpected also was that essentially all of John's Gospel was voted in the 'black', that is, little was found to be the voice of Jesus, especially the many 'I am' statements.

Borg has his own take on the colour coding. He noted that the formal definition of the colours could be presented in more colloquial language as follows:

- Red: 'That's Jesus!'
- Pink: 'Sure sounds like him.'
- Grey: 'Well, maybe.'
- Black: 'There's been some mistake.'

He also indicated that he would himself have put many of the majority of the grey votes into the pink or red column. One eye-catching note was that within the seminar, not only were the members not agreed about everything, they were not unanimous on anything apart from the black votes. Hence his point that on the whole the seminar results need to be seen as the current view of a particular group of Jesus scholars. As such they have considerable value in the teaching enterprise of the church. They underscore our increasingly accepted view of the Gospels in that they contain a profile of 'the developing traditions of the early Christian movement" dated forty to seventy years after the death of Jesus.

Using an archaeological metaphor, Borg presents the Gospels as having two layers. There is the very early one – closer to the time of Jesus – which he calls the pre-Easter Jesus. This layer contains *the voice of Jesus*. Here we find a flesh and blood human being executed by the empire. Then there is the second layer: a post-Easter Jesus who brings *'the voice of the later Christian community'*. This voice refers to what he became to the community which developed after him. It does not refer to the 'finite mortal human being and (the Gospels) can't be considered as historical reports that can be believed about the words and doings of Jesus'.[128] This material comes to us from the last third of the first century and gives us the various writers' modification of his sayings.

Borg indicates these are the community's memories of Jesus and report on their 'understanding of the significance and role of Jesus in their own lives in their own time'.[129] To them he was a 'living spiritual reality who increasingly was seen as having all the qualities of God'. Borg doubts that Jesus ever saw himself the way they did: Word of God, Lamb of God, Light of the World, Son of God, Alpha and Omega. They are not titles he ever gave to himself.

However, at this point, Borg goes where many of his Jesus Seminar fellows did not and could not go. In a surprising move, he invites us to continue to use the established language about Jesus. Seminar members wanted a new language, new thought forms, new creedal statements. He proposes that we see those Word of God and Lamb of God titles as metaphor. Borg wants to *metamorphose* them. He writes that, as a Christian, he affirms these metaphors to be true. He does see Jesus as 'Messiah as the Son of God, the Word of God, the Wisdom/Sophia of God'.[130] Those affirmations are a 'defining element' of what it means to be a Christian. They portray Jesus as 'the decisive revelation or disclosure of God'.

But, in what could be seen as each-way bet, Borg advocates that we employ other language when talking about the historical Jesus, the Jesus before Easter. He calls it a non-messianic way to envisage Jesus and proposes five possibilities: spirit person, healer, wisdom teacher, social prophet and movement initiator. He gets these 'broad strokes' from cross cultural study on types of religious personalities. He provides a radical shorthand for the five: *Jesus as Jewish-mystic*. It is his alternative to Funk's *subversive sage*.

Both Borg and Funk are of one mind: their reconstructions of the historical Jesus are based on their red and pink material. They are not speculating. Their conclusions arise from what they claim are results of the Seminar's biblical research and its interpretation of what is the original voice of Jesus. Yes, it would have been better if there were some written material from Jesus rather than having to use historical and literary research, but that is not how it was. As for why Jesus did not write anything down, Borg notes that he lived in a preliterate and preprint culture. Probably 95 percent or more of those in his times couldn't read what we now know of as the Old Testament or the as-yet-to-be written New Testament. Besides, his audience was the peasant class, agricultural and manual labourers, who made up 90 percent of rural population he travelled to and in. A compelling reason, Borg notes, for Jesus to use his arresting aphorisms and provocative parables.

Borg continues to be a popular author for those interested in recent scholarship on Jesus. His various writings provide a big picture view of Jesus studies in the last 150 years. He writes of a renaissance in biblical studies, marked not only by new methods but also new results. He sees various emerging trends as symptomatic of a new consensus. One is that the view of Jesus as an eschatological prophet – essentially a kingdom of God preacher – is now a minority view in scholarship. Texts critical of this view are now understood as not likely to be his. The second trend is that Jesus was a teacher of subversive wisdom. This profile of him has been reinforced by significant new material now emerging about the social world of Jesus which is providing new ways of understanding the context of his preaching and activity.

Some readers, for example, will be intrigued by Borg's extensive study of the patriarchal structure of Jesus' times, how pervasive it was, and how so many of the Jesus stories involved his 'ignoring and subverting the structures of patriarchy'. Borg notes that the Book of Proverbs is a classic example of the male way of seeing the world. In that book, we find numerous references to the difficult or fretful wife, but none about difficult husbands. 'Adoring portraits of the "ideal wife" are there too, but none of the ideal husband.' The explanation is obvious. This was a book written by men for men. Male images dominate about the deity. Laws are written from a male point of view. Males occupy the official positions in religion.

In Borg's view, Jesus 'challenged the existing order and advocated an alternative'.[131] He sees this challenge as 'political' in the broad sense of the word, involving social criticism, an alternative social vision and what he describes as the 'embodiment of that vision in the life of the community'.[132] Jesus, he claims, was political in three ways.[133] He championed the cause of the exploited peasantry that existed in his times, not by leading a revolt but by engaging in social criticism of the élites of his day. Second, his narrative challenged the patriarchal structure. Third, he mounted a pointed critique of the *purity society* of his day.

On these issues of peasantry, patriarchy and purity, Jesus walked to the beat of a different drum, Borg proposes. He had an alternative social vision which he spelled out in his sayings and were embodied in both his lifestyle and the embryonic communities that grew up around him. Borg sees him as an Elijah-type figure: an ecstatic, a healer, a social prophet and an enlightened one.

Chapter 12

Jesus according to the feminists

An alternative to patriarchal religion

Elizabeth Schussler Fiorenza: *the red sweater wo/men*

Fiorenza vividly remembers wearing that red sweater, knitted for her by her mother. On day one of the first semester of her Ph.D. studies, she found herself surrounded by a sea of about 120 to 150 black- or grey-robed fellow theological students. The professor entered the room with the greeting: *Meine Damen und Herren* (Ladies and Gentlemen), at which point everyone turned and looked at her. She never wore that red sweater again.

The first woman to undertake the full theological program at the University of Wurzburg, Germany, Fiorenza decided to undertake a doctorate, also the first for a woman. In 1944, as a six-year-old, she had fled with her parents away from the Russian army as it advanced through her homeland. Eventually settling in Munster and much influenced by the Second Vatican Council, she decided to become a theologian. During her doctoral program, by which time she had already published a book, her initial scholarship money ran out. Enquiring of her Professor about further funding she was told that he had only three available scholarships and since she had 'no future in theology', he would be giving them to those who did.[134]

Perhaps overcoming this gender bias was at least part of the fuel which sustained her career as a Catholic feminist biblical scholar, a prolific author of theological texts and the holder of prestigious academic appointments in Germany and the USA. In 1984, she was one of the 97 theological persons who signed *A Catholic Statement on Pluralism and Abortion* which invited discussion within that Church on one of its most contentious issues. Worldwide, she conducted workshops and accepted speaking engagements, including in Australia, where she was sponsored by The Australian Feminist Theological Foundation. Several of her books are available at Melbourne's marvellous Dalton McCaughey and Mannix Libraries.

Sophia is her preferred word for God and, claims Fiorenza, Jesus is her prophet. She notes that this ancient word for *wisdom* can be used in religious literature either as a quality a person possesses or as a figuration of the Divine. Although some in the ancient goddess traditions did use the Sophia word to present their deity as fully female, Fiorenza indicates she has no interest in replacing a male God with a goddess or a female God. But she does favour incorporating into her images of God the female concept of wisdom. She notes that when the Hebrew Scriptures referred to God as Wisdom they used the feminine grammatical form. Thus, *Divine Sophia* points to one who is wise in character and feminine in configuration. Readers not familiar with biblical writers use of feminine language for God – in this case Sophia – might try, for starters, to read Proverbs 8 in the Old Testament.

Fiorenza recognises that the Divine Wisdom-Sophia may not be well known or worshipped in mainstream Christianity, but she claims this way of envisaging God has a 'foothold in the Christian Scriptures'.[135] She also points out that there are two other significant ways of imaging God in the Old Testament using feminine grammar: 'Presence' (*Shekhinah*) and 'Spirit' (*Ruach*).[136] Three common biblical names for God and all feminine.

Writing several decades ago on this issue, she was also aware that the female figure of Wisdom for the divine is not accepted by all in biblical scholarship and seldom among conservatives. Indeed, she notes, some women from that branch of Christendom have lost jobs because of their support for any form of feminising God.[137] She notes also that Catholic feminine theologians are more likely than Protestants to draw attention to the female status of Sophia. A major reason for this is that some of the biblical books which present this profile of God appear in the Catholic but not the Protestant Bible. The Book of Wisdom, for example, which does strongly feature God as wisdom in the feminine form, is one such among the collection of around fourteen others, called the *Apocrypha* (dated between 400-200 BC), which the Protestant Bible excludes from its official Sacred Book.

Fiorenza presents God – her Divine Sophia – as *a* 'cosmic figure' who delights in the dance of creation, a teacher of justice, a leader of her people whom she accompanies on their journey, especially those struggling against injustice and/or seeking liberation. She can raise her voice in public places in a 'very unladylike', manner, calling to anyone who will hear her. 'She transgresses boundaries, celebrates life, and nourishes those who will become her friends. Her cosmic house is without walls and her table is set for all.'[138] Fiorenza takes pains to present her view of Divine Wisdom as inclusive. She is at work among 'all people, cultures and religions'.

Fiorenza coined the word *wo/men* to reinforce this inclusiveness. On the one hand, it is her way of presenting the challenge to see women differently. This word is free from gender stereotyping with all the unwelcome consequences of viewing them as ladies, wives, seductresses, subservients, etc. She likes the bumper sticker that asserts that '*Feminism is the radical notion that wo/men are people*'. Women ought not to be seen through the lens of gender language. They are persons. She also makes the point that wo/men 'are not a unitary group and do not have a feminine nature and essence in common.'[139] Nor are they a different species from men. They come in all shapes and sizes. Her new word – wo/men –comes as a challenge to 'think twice' about the language we use. For the same reason she employs s/he and fe/male in order to be inclusive of the male. She is even ready to use the word wo/men as inclusive of men.

Some of them need liberating too. These are the subaltern men, since they do not 'share the élite male privilege'.

Her emphasis on inclusiveness – all are welcomed by Divine Wisdom – leads her further to the image of the wisdom community as 'a society of the co-equals', one of her most famous and provocative statements. Such a society exists in stark contrast to systems characterised by domination and submission. She labels them as *Kyriarchy* which in Greek times was the rule of the lord, the slave-master, the husband, the propertied, the élite freeborn. But *kyriarchy* is also evident in modern, democratised institutions, including Christianity, she insists. They are 'complex pyramidal political systems characterised by superiority and inferiority ... dominance and submission'. Fiorenza's alternative is the Ekklesia of Wo/men – her society of co-equals — 'the congress of full decision-making citizens'.[140]

Reaction to Fiorenza's viewpoints and language range from hostility to delight. The hostiles are unhappy because her material is too radical, too novel, too unbiblical, and employs language that is consumer-unfriendly. Some also see it as another example of feminist drivel, although they could never say that out loud, except behind closed doors with fellow male believers. Those who are delighted, embrace her ideas for a variety of reasons. Chief of these is that they are in accord with their own view of church institutions as hierarchical and patriarchal, to which some would also add bureaucratic and/or dysfunctional.

But what about her Jesus? Again, the hostiles are unhappy and the supporters delighted. Fiorenza sees Jesus as the messenger and prophet of Sophia. His task it is to 'proclaim the oracles of Sophia'.[141] He did exist and he saw himself in that long line of Jewish prophets. He did not initiate nor close that line, but he was certainly one of its 'eminent' members. She finds no evidence to support assertions of 'exclusivity or superiority' on Jesus' part. Nor does she take the view that his death was 'willed' or 'intended' by Sophia.

As messenger of Sophia, Jesus' prophetic task was to 'gather together the children of Israel to their gracious Sophia',[142] and to announce that the Kingdom is open to all. She claims that the earliest Gospel material asserts again and again that Jesus claimed the Kingdom for three distinct types of people.[143] One is the destitute poor. Her view is that Jesus saw poverty as injustice, not personal failure. The second group include the sick and crippled. The third group are tax collectors, sinners and prostitutes. Since God is always on the side of those who are trampled down all three groups are God's concern.

Fiorenza is captured by the Jesus parables that stress God's inclusiveness. In them Sophia is likened to a woman diligently searching her house for a lost coin (Luke 13), or the assertive widow demanding justice (Luke 18), or the baker woman whose activity it is to leaven the bread (Luke 13). In both his utterances and deeds, Jesus gives high priority to the poor, the disenfranchised, the ostracised women of his times. She asserts that the early Jesus movement proclaimed a society 'free of domination (that) does not exclude anyone'.[144] The Kingdom message Jesus proclaimed envisaged a world that was 'free of hunger, poverty and domination. It summoned the people in the local villages, the sinners, tax collectors, debtors, beggars, prostitutes and all those wo/men exploited and marginalised'.[145]

In her view, the early Jesus movement was egalitarian: a fellowship of equals. She does not, however, believe that his stance for the poor and concern for women was a strategy for structural change. What he does is to 'subvert them by envisaging a different future and different human relationships on the grounds that all persons are created by their Jesus' Sophia-God'.[146]

But she also claims that it didn't take long for his original message and the community itself to morph into something else. Jesus begins to be understood and portrayed as more than the messenger of Sophia. They gave him what she calls 'grammatically masculine Christological titles such as *kyrios* and *soter* (lord and saviour)'.[147] Emancipating him from such dogmas was clearly part of the task Fiorenza set herself, just as Jesus, in her view, set himself the Sophaic task of emancipating those around him.

In summary, Fiorenza is arguing for a different God image and Jesus story than the one so heavily influenced by the structure and language of the Roman Empire and feudal society, which emphasised fatherhood, great monarchs or overlords, male authority, absolute power vested in few and hierarchical structures. She seeks a feminine incorporation into the image of God which celebrates inclusiveness, justice, equality and acceptance and rejects a perpetuation of womanhood conceived in terms of submission, service, motherhood, dependence self-abnegation, beauty and helplessness. She dubbed this the Cult of True Womanhood, a profile which legitimatises the exclusion of women from positions of power.

Unsurprisingly, Fiorenza has a novel take on the use of Christianity's famous symbol of the Cross. Like most feminist scholars, she rejects interpretations of Jesus' death on the Cross as a necessary salvation act of sacrifice: one man – God's own loved Son – bearing the sins of the world in his own body. She supports those who aim to retell the Jesus story in a way that does not emphasise self-sacrifice, obedience, suffering for others, sacrificial love, so often promoted as the way women ought to see themselves. For women who have been victimised or abused by fathers or other males, to have Christianity presenting a story of a divine child being punished by the divine Father does not sit well. Fiorenza prefers to present the Easter passion story in terms of an unjust execution. For her, the Cross challenges us to 'protest the imperial powers of victimisation and injustice that shape both our society and our religion'.[148]

She writes approvingly of witnessing a Good Friday demonstration which paraded a fifty-foot banner asking the question: 'Were You There When They Crucified the Poor?' This image led her to the opinion that the crucifixion story should be told in terms different from those associated with blood atonement. She advised that we 'keep the Cross as a symbol of injustice for poor welfare mothers;

for brutalised or murdered black men and women; for women seeking the right to make their own decisions about reproduction'.

Elizabeth A. Johnson: *She Who Is*

Three years younger than Fiorenza, Johnson's academic life and religious offerings paralleled hers in many ways. The title of her very readable book *She Who Is* speaks vividly of her passion for incorporating female imagery into the language used about God. Like Fiorenza, she is appalled that Jesus' death has been portrayed as required by God as repayment for sin. In her view, any who enter into solidarity with those who suffer or are victimised are liable to come to this end. Like Fiorenza, she sees Jesus as an *envoy of Sophia*. Jesus is *Personified Wisdom*.

Born 7 December 1941 into an Irish Catholic family, the eldest of seven children, Johnson grew up in Brooklyn, New York, and became the first woman to earn a Ph.D. degree at the Catholic University of America. She retired in 2018 as Distinguished Professor Emerita of Theology at Fordham University, a Jesuit institution in New York, where she taught for many years, having published fifteen or more books, received various academic awards and chaired two Theological Societies in the USA.

Controversy, of course, surrounded her. In 2007, she published *Quest for the Living God* in which she detailed what she saw as a renaissance of new ideas about God which had taken place in the middle of 20th century. The book did not please the Committee of Doctrine of the United States Conference of Catholic Bishops. In 2011, they declared that *Quest for the Living God* did not correspond with authentic Christian Teaching. She also displeased some Bishops by suggesting that Mary was not 'humble and obedient'. I read *She Who Is* in 1996 and have often gone back to it. *Library Journal*, an Americans publication for librarians, declared it 'Perhaps the best book of feminist theology to date'.

In this work, Johnson argues that the historic male formulations about God have done much to suppress and exclude women. She describes this as the 'masculinisation of God'.[149] Consequently, female images in speech about God have been ruled out and Jesus as a man has been used to tie a tight knot between maleness and divinity. She points out that the word *God* is not an easy one to discard. Some have stayed with it by preference. Some have tried dropping it without success. Others have taken the path she has, that of cleansing the word of its various defilements or mutilations. She asserts that there is a 'plethora' of names and images for God in the Bible, some non-personal, some masculine and some feminine. She argues for the legitimacy of them all, not for one triumphing over the others, specifically 'a narrow focus on one or two patriarchal symbols'.[150]

Johnson favours the term Sophia for God – a feminine figure – as a symbol for a mothering/nurturing God. She notes some in her feminist scholarship group have proposed God/ess or God/She. They do not appeal to her. And, following Fiorenza, she draws attention to the use of feminine grammar for some of the biblical language about God, specifically for the terms Wisdom, Spirit and Presence.

Further, Johnson points out that the Bible contains a vast array of female symbols for God and God's activity in the world which come from the woman's experiences of bearing, birthing, feeding and nursing infants. God is also portrayed as a midwife and a comforting mother. Johnson asks that these images be seen as central to who God is. She also reminds us that this female personification is not just about her as a mother or a sister or a female friend. She is also 'liberator, establisher of justice, judge, preacher, chef and hostess and a myriad of other female roles'.[151]

She claims that Jesus used 'a riot of images' to depict God and God's way of dealing with humans. His language about God is diverse and colourful, especially in his parables: a woman searching for money, a travelling businessman, a shepherd, an employer, a baker woman, all existing alongside his well-recognised designation of God as Father (*Abba*). Her general view about Jesus' language is that whenever we can have confidence that it is him speaking, it is to emphasise compassion for those who are suffering.

She is very excited about Jesus, as most Jesus liberators seem to be, and equally forthright about what she asserts are the historic distortions of him. As with Fiorenza, for example, she can't believe the significance of Jesus' death so often presented by the theologians of the church. She writes: 'Feminist theology repudiates any interpretation of the death of Jesus as required by God in repayment of sin'.[152] Only an angry sadistic father would require such a thing, *the very worst kind of male behaviour*. Her take on the crucifixion is that those who enter into solidarity with the victimised and suffering will often find themselves violated or destroyed.

What equally annoys her is that maleness has been used to justify domination and reinforce a patriarchal image of God. If Jesus is a male and reveals God, then this at the very least points *to* 'maleness as an essential characteristic of divine being itself'.[153] This may not indicate a strict identification but it certainly orientates divinity to maleness rather than to femaleness. That the male sex is chosen for the enfleshment of God strengthens the perception that 'a particular honour, dignity, and normativity accrues to the male sex',[154] and provides more evidence to use in promoting the case that men are suited to the priesthood but women are not. That the Word might have become female flesh 'is not even seriously imaginable'.[155]

That Jesus was a male human being is not, she notes, in question. This does not concern her, nor would it have worried her if the role of Jesus had been played by a female. He was a male and he did live and he was a Jewish prophet, and yes, he did use a paternal metaphor for God by the use of the word Father (*Abba*). Describing God this way surely contributed to the normalising of God as Male and shutting the gate on the use of other nomenclature.

But Johnson makes the case that although the tradition after Jesus moved that way, it was not so with Jesus himself. She claims the parental metaphor of God as Father is attributed to Jesus a whole lot less in the earlier written Gospels than the later ones. Only four times in Mark, the first written, and 15 in Luke; 49 in Matthew and 109 in John, the final gospel. In other words, the church in the last decades of the first century made far more of the paternal nature of God than did Jesus himself. Perhaps this was inevitable, given that the early church emerged in a Greco-Roman world model of patriarchal household and the language of empire. But it was not only Jesus' language for God that was distorted. So too was he. Jesus is cast as imperial Christ, the Head of the family and the Church, to whom obedience is owed. Not good news for the exploited, the oppressed, the marginalised, as the Latin American liberation theologians pointed out.[156]

Jesus' speech about God, she claims, is considerably varied, revealing far less paternalism than is generally attributed to him. She sees his language as diverse and colourful, not monolithic. Certainly not what the later church attributes to him. She describes that as a distortion of the original Jesus. Johnson does not dispute that Jesus did use the word *Abba* for God, but claims this designation brings to the fore the sense of intimacy Jesus felt existed between him and God, not a defining of the maleness of the other.

Johnson's writing, sometimes academic and technical as befits a scholar, can also can be poetic and inspiring. For example, she writes of God 'plunging into sinful human history and transforming from within',[157] a vivid metaphor for the traditional doctrine of incarnation. Or this: 'She becomes flesh, choosing the very stuff of the cosmos as her own personal reality forever. She thereby becomes irrevocably, physically connected to the human adventure, for better or worse'.[158]

Then there is her characterisation of Jesus as the *envoy of Sophia*. He is the one who *enfleshes* (another favourite word of hers) the plunge. He is the prophet who announces that God is inclusive love, a God who wills 'humanity and wholeness', especially, Johnson notes, for the 'poor and heavy burdened'.[159] His task is to gather the outcast under the wings of their gracious

Sophia-God. He is the envoy of Sophia who 'walks the paths of justice and peace and invites others to do the same'. She writes that Jesus 'delights in being with people; joy, insight and a sure way to God are found in his company'.[160] His table, she continues, is inclusive of 'the most disvalued, even tax collectors, sinners and prostitutes'. She looks forward to the day when Christian theology is not so interested in the maleness of Jesus but 'the scandal of his option for the poor and the marginalised'.[161]

Sally Douglas: *Woman Wisdom*

Australia has had a long line of feminist theologians but, unsurprisingly, they were mostly required to do their work outside the mainline seminaries. That some theological colleges have opened the doors to them in recent times is a welcome sign. One symbol of that change was a recent joint book launch by two theological authors, the Reverend Dr Sally Douglas and the Reverend Associate Professor, Robyn Whitaker, academics at Pilgrim Theological College, part of the UCA Centre for Theology and Ministry in Melbourne. Both were interviewed in the October 2023 edition of *Crosslight*, a bi-monthly magazine put out by the Uniting Church Synod of Victoria and Tasmania. *Even the Devil Quotes Scripture* is the title of Whitaker's book and Douglas called hers *Jesus Sophia*. Her chosen audience is clearly not academia but the ordinary folk of the local parish, an institution she clearly has a great love for, one which I once saw her shed tears for.

Douglas acknowledges the work of Fiorenza and Johnson in recovering the concept of Sophia in biblical studies in the 1980s and 1990s, especially their work on the Old Testament references to the female divine figure Wisdom, Woman Wisdom or Sophia. But as she became more acquainted with her research on the issue she was shocked 'to discover that again and again Jesus is imaged as her'.[162] She insists that not only did the early church communities celebrate Jesus as the female divine, so too the early church writers. Her easy-to-read 160-page book is both a presentation of Jesus as

Woman Wisdom and an exploration of what, as she put it, this might mean for how we live today. Each of her chapters concludes with she calls Wondering Questions followed by a General Prayer and finally a Prayer for Specific Occasions or Parts of the Day.

One of her big themes is that in Jesus the fullness of God is expressed. She attributes more divinity to Jesus than Funk, and none of the male masculinity of orthodox theology. Her biblical studies led her to the conviction that Jesus is the 'female divine embodied in a person'.[163] The early sections of her book are devoted to the prevailing feminist exposition of the various ways the Old Testament authors imaged God as female. The use of the grammatically feminine word *Hokmah* as a designation for God is a foremost example of this. This word literally means wisdom. Douglas strongly objects to the standard biblical scholarship's translating the word 'it'. Why disguise God's womanliness by using gender-neutral language she asks or, worse still, referring to God as 'he'?

She makes the same claim about the various New Testament references to Jesus as Wisdom. They ought also to be translated in the Greek feminine word Sophia, thus designating Jesus as woman wisdom, hence the title of her book *Jesus Wisdom*. And she insists this feminisation of Jesus would have been taken for granted in Jesus' times and for the decades that immediately followed his death. She discusses the New Testament passages that refer to Jesus as Wisdom and makes the case that if some of the Gospel and Epistle authors do not offer explanations about this identification, the reason is that first century readers were quite familiar with that way of interpreting the word Wisdom.

Her earlier publication is very strong on this. She rejects the view of scholars like Funk and Bultmann, and most others in recent biblical scholarship, that Jesus was slowly *escalated* from being 'charismatic man' into a 'God one', in the second and third centuries after his death.[164] Her view is that Jesus was 'understood and celebrated as the *female divine*' from the earliest strands of the Christian traditions. Her book is committed to justifying this viewpoint.

Douglas variously describes Jesus as the God One, as Sophia Christ, as Jesus Sophia, as the Holy Human One. She also calls him the Divine One. In Jesus as Sophia the fullness of God had been expressed. Commenting on a segment found in the 60 AD book of Colossians (1:15-20) she asserts that '... this hymn demonstrates that very early, before church buildings are even dreamt of, Jesus is celebrated as the God One.'[165] But not, she continues, as a warrior god-king, as in the imagery of the Roman Empire, nor Christianity's construction of God as an old man on a cloud. What was being celebrated was the 'female divine embodied in person.' There is no fire and brimstone in his profile either, she continues, this Sophia Christ delights in humanity and embodies hospitality, feasting with and welcoming all kinds of people, including those deemed to be low lives.

Douglas proffers no limp Jesus. Her Jesus is an angry Jesus 'in whom the fierce compassion of the divine' is demonstrated exposing evil and injustice and dismantling hierarchies. In the Gospels, Jesus gets angry, says hard and annoying things to all kinds of people, confronts those who are misusing their power. And, Douglas claims, whereas in the Bible it is possible for the female divine Sophia to express anger, women in patriarchal cultures are not given the same freedom.

In her chapter on anger, she also invites a reconsideration of the Cross of Jesus. Not for her a God who 'craves blood' in sacrifice, God a sadistic father who needs his son to suffer. Such theories lead many people to reject Christianity, she notes. From the perspective of Sophia, the Cross begins with the incarnation. Jesus Sophia, she writes 'chooses to walk towards us in person ... even though she has seen our violence toward her emissaries and understands the risks'.[166] The violence of the Crucifixion is perpetrated by humans: 'a legally sanctioned murder meted out on the God One'. The violence is ours. But if we are confronted by our own violence, we are also confronted by 'the astonishing compassion of God'. Divine non-retaliation may look like weakness, but it is stronger than all violence. Resurrection life 'rescues us and scoops us up into her love'.

The gift of divine friendship figures large in religious outlook of Douglas. She quotes the biblical passage in John 15 in which, in his farewell speech to his disciples, Jesus tells them that he does not call them servants but friends. Being friends with Jesus can, she notes, be problematic in churches with patriarchal systems of governance. Friendship is threatening to those in power in these institutions. And friendship can also slip into sentimentality, for example in the saccharine music and imagery found in some Christian churches. Moreover, she continues, divine friendship is not simply about our personal nourishment. Such friendship also draws us out of ourselves and into 'the divine's wild compassion for all'.

Breastfeeding is another of Douglas's challenging ideas. She quotes 1 Peter 2:2-3 where the Jesus communities are invited to imagine themselves breastfeeding from Christ: 'Like new-born infants, long for the pure, spiritual milk so that by it you may grow into salvation, if indeed you have tasted that the Lord is good'. There is convincing evidence elsewhere, which she supplies, to support her view that in this breastfeeding metaphor Jesus is understood as Sophia. She also claims that although contemporary biblical scholars gloss over this image, the early church writers such as Clement, born 150 AD, an important teacher and theologian of the early church, didn't. 1000 years later another famous theologian, Julian of Norwich did the same.

Douglas writes of her own experience of feeding a tiny baby from her own body and of the 'unmistakable overlaps' in the themes of self-giving and sustenance that can be found in both breastfeeding and the act of the taking in of the body of Christ in the Eucharist liturgy. Douglas notes that this image of breastfeeding from Christ may be a shock to some and perhaps also startling to discover there was a time it was openly used by theologians, including at Holy Communion. She writes that this is understandable, given that male language and imagery for God has gained the ascendency across denominations while female divine imagery has been downplayed, suppressed and ignored.

Douglas enjoys a dual career as academic and pastor. I thoroughly enjoyed reading her book not only because of her scholarly advocacy for Jesus as divine wisdom but also her Prayers and Wondering Thoughts.

My view about feminist theology

I was raised in the male-dominated theological scene. None of my lecturers at my two-year Bible College was female. Only one of the two score academic staff at the Princeton Theological Seminary in New Jersey, where I did my Bachelor of Divinity (1962-65), was a woman. She taught religious education classes for those women intending to take up a position in the religion departments of one of those vast American congregations. And, as I recall, I had only one woman lecturer at Otago University, Dunedin NZ where I completed my Bachelor of Arts in 1958-60. She taught Greek language. Nor did I ever see a woman in clerical robes at any time in those Dunedin undergraduate days nor during my three-year Presbyterian Parish appointment in New Zealand in 1968-71.

The idea that God could be imaged and described in other than a masculine profile was seldom on the drawing board. The concept of feminist theology was never mentioned in the years 1962-65 when I trained at Princeton. Fiorenza was only twenty-six that time. Sally Douglas wasn't born. And during most of my work life as a parish minister in three localities – Texas USA, Dunedin NZ and Melbourne Australia – women were non-existent or had an extraordinarily low profile in the denominational structures above the local level. Noteworthy that even now (2023), of the sixteen Presidents of the General Assembly in the UCA, only three have been women, of whom one only was ordained.

One of my few regrets about being a clergy person was that from the time of commencing required studies to become an ordained clergyman, it took forty-one years before I read a serious book of theology written by a woman; Johnson's *She Who Is*. For various reasons, I am now a strong supporter of feminist theology. It has so much to offer those seeking an alternative presentation of Jesus of Nazareth. Their Jesus is some kind of spiritual activist, friendly, sagacious, quite unconcerned about self-promotion, often enigmatic, and always inclusive. He is unquestionably gripped by some primordial disposition to advance the welfare of those who have been disempowered or side-lined or abused.

I agree with the feminine case that much of traditional theology has been founded on the proposition that women are less: less able, less intelligent, less resourceful, less stable, less gifted, less lots of things. I admire their scholarly perseverance in uncovering what the males covered up: the feminine impulse at work so decisively in those early days of the Jesus story. And I like it that they are much distressed about a punitive God who requires some retributive pay off in order to stop being angry.

There is also a freshness and excitement about some of the language they use to promote their vision of God. They may be gentle rebels, but they are not heretics. Like many adventurers in the land of theology they are respectful of the great creeds of historic Christianity, but see them as dated documents from former eras. Their work advances the agenda of many who argue that each era must provide its own answers to the questions of who Jesus was and how to envisage the way God acts in the world.

Part 3

Real people, real dilemmas

What follows are the musings/reflections/conclusions of six Baby Boomers, whom I invited to write an 800 word something about their experience of religion. All are friends of mine from over several decades.

Had Henry James written his famous Varieties of Religious Experience in the present era, he would have had good cause to include their contributions in his collection about the diverse pathways that personal religion traverses. They illustrate the changing panorama of individual's religious beliefs and values over the decades. Theirs is a story of evolution, adaption, modification. Minor tinkering here and there for some. Full-scale abandonment by others. A task compete for some. A work in progress for others. Various emotions are on display here too: delight, angst, rage, confusion, boredom, gratitude. They certainly illustrate that Christianity has been a poisoned chalice for some but a safe, enriching guide for others.

I love what they have written.

Brace Bateman
Thank you, Christianity

(Retired Minister of Religion)

I appreciate Christianity for several reasons.

It encourages me to be generous. Without it, I would hold on to what I have and not give some of it away. It says, 'Brace, share'. And as I do this (after a while), I feel really good about not clinging on to what I have, but instead sharing.

Forgiveness is fantastic. I err, we all do, but it is wonderful to speak the error to the divine one within myself, and then let it go off with the winds.

I have heard in church that I am a Son of God. That is amazing. It certainly makes me feel better about myself than anything else could. Then I couple these last two together (that I err and that I am free.) That gives me a true and valued self-perception.

Prayer is excellent. Why? The quietness. The being connected in a way with God.

Christianity suggests I go to where other Christians occasionally gather: church. Singing there feels good. Someone up the front leading me in prayer opens me to some wonderful thoughts. Making a few new friends there is excellent, partly because they are on the look-out for new friendships too.

In an ironic twist of fate what can sometimes precipitate a re-visiting and re-working of our religion can be our non-church adult children. My mum grew up in the era when women only ever wore dresses. It was just what you did. I never heard her express a view to my sister when in her late twenties she started to wear trousers. But Mum one day made the switch. As for the religious clothes they dressed in, they were peas in the same pod.

Singing feels good. I never sing alone around my home or work-place.

Reading the Christian Bible is a mixed blessing; sometimes I get wonderful benefit, other times I get nothing at all from it.

I like the Christ-figure. What a man, what a figure he was. Hooray!!

And thank you for reading through this little writing.

John Coulson
So, What of Jesus?

(Retired civil engineer, UCA elder)

The older I get, the more I realise religion is about caring: that is what it was for Jesus.

It started when I was about six or eight, sitting in church with my Mum, Dad in the church choir on the other side. The well-respected minister told us that Jesus came alive again on the third day. I'm daydreaming up to this point and am startled. People don't come live again. Once our pet cats and dogs have died, they stay dead. The minister can't be believed about this subject.

In my late teens, I think that the New Testament stories of Jesus' early years have no merit since it wasn't until he was nearly thirty that he became noticed by the community and the stuff they then recalled about his early years is very suspect.

The gospels are full of quotations of dialogue, and after many youth group games of forming a long line and providing a short, detailed message to the person at one end who whispers it to the next person; the message at the other end is unintelligibly garbled. The dialogue in the gospels, written forty to sixty years later, even with earlier supporting information, can't be in any way accurate.

The Bible was written to help people understand the world they lived in. The mass of human knowledge was very limited. Over the past 2000 years – much longer for the Old Testament stuff – the extent of human knowledge has mushroomed enormously. We now know whither the wind blows and can forecast it, with surprising accuracy, for up to seven days ahead. Also, we know about electricity, magnetism, atoms and so on, but since we don't know what we don't know, there is still a lot to know and understand. But there is no such thing as magic. There is a rational demonstrable explanation for everything; even stuff we can't explain yet. Such as where did the universe come from?

So, what of the Jesus story?

We humans need a story to help us cope with living in a community. It seems to me clear that the Old Testament is a guide to how to get on with one another. Jesus appears to have been smarter than some and figured that myriads of rules are not enough. Better to have some simple guiding principles rather than rigidly following rules.

His recorded life shows him 'caring' for needy people. No magic, but remarkable results. It shows him caring for all sorts of people, lepers, blind men, hated tax collectors, foreigners. He also notes that caring for others is tough; forgiving others, not seven times but seventy times seven.

Jesus also was very critical of the established 'Church' professionals. He clearly thought they had lost the plot, although he never attempted to start an opposition church.

Thus, there is no foundation for any of the Church practices – Christmas, the lord's prayer, communion – other than it helps with my 'community'.

As babies, we are programmed, and quickly learn, that if we want something for our well-being – food, nappy changing, warmth – we'd better yell about it. Having learnt this early it is hard as we grow up to put self aside in favour of 'others'; to become mature adults. Girls learn this early, with their dolls; and, rapidly, on becoming mothers. Blokes, much favoured by their mums, take a long time to mature, and many never do.

Our congregations are gatherings of people with similar 'caring' beliefs, whom we respect and who gather together to reinforce, in each other, the intent to keep on caring in spite of the difficulties.

Faced with a choice between (1) benefit to me and (2) benefit to another, it is hard to always choose for 'the other'. The institutional churches miss the point. They think forgiving is because we have been naughty. Evil does not exist. There is a continuum between zero caring and total care and individuals behave – for each event – somewhere along this continuum, all the time. When I fall short of this intent, I need to start again afresh; forgiven; not beat myself about the head because I am not perfect.

The present-day institutional Church fails, as it did in Jesus' time, because it is mostly run by blokes, and groups mostly adopt the most beneficial position for the group. It still misses the point and so is the pits.

More recently, I agonise about the image of God. In Australia, we don't comprehend lords, or rulers and the concept of Father is outdated and some don't find it helpful. My feeble brain finally clicked that if there are a billion stars in each galaxy and a billion galaxies, then the god of the universe is not comprehensible by me. It is okay for a sparrow to fall and be counted, but if that sparrow is unable to then fly it will be eaten by a circling hawk or whatever.

So, what of Jesus, who seemed pretty smart, has a contribution. He said' that 'anyone who has seen me has seen the father'; and also 'He that has done this to the least of these my brothers and sisters has done it to me'.

God is the 'spirit' in each of us, the sort of 'ideal' that we all can perceive we should try to achieve. We need to 'worship' each other; hence the opening paragraph.

Simon Harvey
Embracing my doubt, finding my freedom

(Educationalist, Musician, Therapist)

For many years, I was embarrassed to say I was raised in the Plymouth (later Exclusive) Brethren, but now I say it with some pride, because I survived intact!

It's hard to pinpoint at what age my Christian castle began to crumble. It began with resentment, progressed to embarrassment, and then struggled through a long period of hesitant conformity until I found enough emotional and intellectual space to examine the foundations. I suppose I'm still on that road today, knocking down many walls but leaving some stakes in the ground.

I actually feel grateful for my Christian upbringing, because it gave me a context or grounding, enabling me to depart from it with some authority and conviction. I'm also incredibly grateful for the love and the space my parents gave me to knock down walls and find real joy and freedom outside the castle, especially because, for most of their lives, they were so steeped in such a dogma-filled and puritanical version of Christianity. I'm fortunate, I know, that the way out of a sectarian straightjacket can be very painful, and the fact that it wasn't painful for me is due to my parents. Some of my cousins who decided to leave the brethren were totally rejected by their parents.

I remember having a conversation with my father as my Christian castle was crumbling. It was about the supposed necessity to accept Jesus as Saviour in order to go to heaven. My question was something like, 'How about all those people in Africa who've never heard of Jesus, why should they go to hell?' My father's answer, to his credit, was simply 'I don't know, son'. That was typical of him – he had no pretence, he was just honest; once I was an adult he never preached at me or pulled rank on me, and I loved and respected him for it.

Today, there's no castle, but there is one prominent stake in the ground, it's a spiritual stake. It marks my awareness of an omnipresent, loving, unifying Presence. This awareness doesn't have anything to do with Jesus (or Buddha or Mohammed, etc); it doesn't have anything to do with believing anything in particular or following certain rituals. This Presence, this Life-Force, this God, is not owned by anyone! The Universe is imbued by this Presence, and we are able to experience it most powerfully as we relate to the Life that surrounds us and sustains us.

Whoops. Sorry if that seems like a sermon. I'm just trying to describe what I feel. I guess that is one of the reasons why conversation about religion can be tricky. If I say what I believe or what I feel (as I just did), and if you don't believe or feel the same, it can be interpreted as a criticism of you. But in this context, such an interpretation is mistaken; we are talking about belief, not logic! We are not dealing with science, we are dealing with belief, feeling, and experience! These are not wrong, they just ARE. Our responsibility, when we are required to describe our perspectives or beliefs, is to attempt to do so as honestly as possible without 'gilding the lily'. I have great respect for those (including some of my siblings) who hold on to what I call the 'mythological' aspects of their faith; what I find challenging is when (or if) that respect is not reciprocated. Some examples of those 'mythological' aspects of Christianity – the virgin birth, salvation through the sacrifice of Jesus (the necessary 'shedding of his blood') – I no longer believe. It is not that I deny the usefulness of myth, ritual, ceremony or symbolism, it is simply that I no longer find them necessary or useful to my spiritual life.

The aspect of religiosity that I find most disturbing is the judgment, hypocrisy, and inconsistency displayed by some religious adherents (not just Christians), particularly the so called 'fundamentalists'.

The belief that I am 'right' and you are 'wrong' – when it comes to expression of religious faith – is judgmental, divisive and dangerous; this makes much sermonising, preaching, and evangelism problematic for me. Preaching that is proselytising or evangelising is tantamount to saying 'get on the right path', whereas preaching that is teaching is about raising issues about life on which one can reflect.

From my perspective, the 'Jesus as Son of God' tenet of Christianity is one of the most divisive, because it is holds up Jesus as unique, as a rung above other 'prophets', the 'Son of God' no less. Again, the implication is 'we are right', so 'you must be wrong', or ours is the real deal, yours is not, or believe this and you have everlasting life, otherwise you are doomed to a so-called 'afterlife' separate from God. In my way of conceptualising it, we are all, including Jesus, 'Sons of God', that is, we are all 'One with God', we are all part of that omnipresent Life Force which is the great unifier and sustainer of life itself.

Sigrid Jacob
My religious /spiritual journey

(Welfare Worker/Nature Lover/Counsellor)

Until the age of five, I mostly lived with my grandparents in a Catholic part of Europe. I loved going to Mass in the baroque village church. I drank in the visual splendour of the church, the processions, rituals, mysterious nuns, scent and smoke of incense, lofty and sublime music of the organ and choir and, seemingly, the entire village filing to the altar for communion. I remember feeling part of something special.

My grandmother taught me to fear God (channelled by thunderstorms when he was angry with me) and that served to regulate my behaviour. In hindsight, I realise that I didn't want to displease her and God didn't exist for me. This grounding set me up to associate church with beauty, grandeur, mystery and ritual. I was subsequently taught Christian history and values by my (non-Catholic) church-attending parents. After each church and Sunday school attendance, we children had to articulate what we had learnt.

I learnt that it was most important to apply the enunciated values in my daily life and didn't think of it as exclusively associated with God or religion. I forgot about a being 'up there somewhere' who was monitoring my behaviour.

When I was about nine years old, my father introduced me to teachings about other faiths, cultures and world peace organisations. I formed the view that they all held similar beliefs and values with the unifying themes of looking out for, and helping, each other, especially disadvantaged people, acceptance of differences and aspirations to be decent human beings.

I left my parents' home at seventeen years old, totally unprepared for functioning outside the family. I rented a room from a family who attended an Assembly of God church. I went along with them, due to wanting their approval and not knowing what else to do with my time. I liked the joyous and vibrant atmosphere, the singing and mystery of speaking in tongues. I saw it as a community, rather than as something to do with God. My church-attending days ended when I met a boyfriend and joined his social group of migrants (like me!)—young folk centred on a soccer club. I had found my community.

I later came to understand how vulnerable people, looking for belonging, acceptance, a family or meaning can become involved with churches (and other organisations and cults) and become reliant on the institution, unquestioning of and loyal to it, even though belonging is conditional on compliance with teachings and behavioural imperatives. I wondered how that could be called religion. Eventually, I realised that religion, as practised by churches (Christian and others), has long had a significant function of providing/enforcing community order and cohesion.

My next step along the journey was to learn Transcendental Meditation in my late 20s, which involved Vedic teachings (of India). This further reinforced my view that humanity has a variety of religious institutions, practices and names for God, whilst sharing common values and the trait of human decency.

I continue to be curious and to explore belief systems and cultures that grab my attention, including those of the Australian indigenous peoples. I am drawn to nature, the arts, anthropology, sociology and psychology. I see congruence, inter-dependence and connectedness between them. Maybe this my religion.

If I look for order in the universe, I draw on a belief of the existence of a 'competency' which is greater than any individual or society, with nature and humanity being expressions of it. I am open to there being no order and that essentially most of 'it' is unknown and unknowable by the senses and by the brain that we use to understand life. It's a nebulous, mysterious thing that I have no wish to clearly define, as that would spoil a key element for me. This is the best that I can do to define 'God'.

I see religion as the practical application and celebration of 'godliness'. Over time, the Anglo-Saxon/Western cultures have increasingly promoted scientific knowledge, personal freedoms and self-responsibility. Our fears of self and others have come to light and we have developed individual and secular understanding, balms and protections. There appears to be decreasing reliance on a 'Heavenly Father' to protect, take responsibility for and forgive us or the weekly pep talk at church, encouraging or exhorting us to goodness.

Perhaps transforming (over centuries) and now declining religious philosophy and practice is part of societal evolution. Curiosity and questioning are no longer treated as threats to society and science has enabled mystery, ignorance and awe to be replaced with factual knowledge.

In contrast to my grandmother, I do not abdicate self-responsibility to the church, which for her was master and security blanket. Regulation has moved from the external to internal, values are learnt and absorbed from non-religious sources, we have many options for belonging and seemingly are less inclined to contemplate.

Anne McClelland
Becoming myself

(Retired English teacher, unapologetic atheist)

I was brought up in a conventional, loving and secure – if circumscribed – God-fearing household. Believing in God, loving Jesus and going to Church and Sunday school were assumed.

The driver behind this was my mother's utter devotion to Christianity and, more particularly, Methodism. Her heroes were John and Charles Wesley and, on Earth, Robert Menzies.

During my teenage years, I began to find all of this, to put it mildly, irksome. Though as yet unarticulated, my doubts were many. Dragged through Sunday school, Church and Christian Endeavour throughout my childhood and teens, I was trapped. I was even dragooned into being a Sunday school teacher. I hated it, but such was my reluctance to upset my mother, I stuck it out.

On Sunday evenings during my last year at school, Mother trotted off to Church for a reinforcing second dose of the day. Her face – as she left my father and me watching the BBC thriller – was tight-lipped and reproachful. Not to go with her was one thing, but to sit watching the recently-acquired ungodly TV was another.

I cannot pinpoint exactly the day I fully acknowledged that I did not believe in God the Father, God the Son and God the Holy Spirit: the whole kit and caboodle. The relief was enormous. I was delighted. I did not seriously regret my prior acquiescence: my mother was much-loved and guileless. Confrontation was unnecessary and would have caused much pain. (She knew, I suspect, in her heart.)

I was free, both to revel in my young life at University and in my newly-discovered atheism. This is not to say that I was 'free' of the precepts drummed into us. We never had 'moods' in our family, we were told, presumably because they were unchristian. We were taught to think of others, not self, and not to feel too pleased with ourselves and our achievements, though it was expected that we be top of the class. We were exhorted to do unto others as we would have them do unto us.

I do not suggest that these family values were anything but pure and purely-intentioned. Even so, they left me self-doubting and insecure. I was quite good at a few things, but always compared myself with others and found myself wanting. At the ripe old age of twenty-three, I married a believer and, until the birth of my first son five years later, toed the newly-acquired family line. Out of the frying pan into the fire. Even worse than eleven o'clock on a freezing Ballarat morning was three o'clock in a tiny, weatherboard, boiling hot Mallee church where the same old rituals prevailed, albeit garbed in Presbyterian rather than Methodist robes. I even played the old wheezy organ (badly) for the hymns. On reflection, I see this as cowardly but, given my upbringing, not surprising. Don't upset anybody.

When my first son arrived, I seized the excuse: it was necessary that I stay at home to look after the baby. No more Church! I was by this time twenty-eight. I was still a mouse, but the lioness was stirring. When the minister called and suggested that I was using my motherhood as a means to avoid his no doubt enlightening sermons, (true of course), I prevaricated. How I wish that I had said, as I would now, 'You're dead right, Mate'. His words had the opposite effect from that which he intended: it crystallised my resentment and my discomfort with my own hypocrisy. I had had it. My two children were never baptised, to the alarm of both sets of parents. I refused to lie.

Why am I an atheist? At one level, it is simply an instinctive conviction. It's a denial of the way in which I was brought up, one which did not ring true. It's a result of observing a nasty world in which religion is arguably a core cause of wars, intolerance, hatred, obsession and sheer crazy pig-headedness. And sexual abuse.

There is no god, not a Christian one or any other sort.

I recognise that the potential for belief in some powerful Being can bring comfort to some people and mitigate the inevitable awareness that we are, essentially, on our own. No-one else, and certainly no omnipresent adviser, is there to do it for us. Family, friends and community all help in negotiating the complexities of life, but in the end, we must rely on our inner resources to balance the scales and make the judgments as to how to proceed.

Do it yourself. No-one can hold your hand.

I used to worry that without some sort of a framework I would not be able to imbue in my children the values I believed they should live by. I think that no longer. Both have a strong ethical sense, both think about and care for others, though not in the soggy way I do. And they are both non-believers. So, too, is my husband, if a little less positively than myself.

The words of the incomparable and uncompromising John Lennon say it all: "Imagine…".

Amanda Swaney
My view on religion

(Educationalist)

At the age of thirteen, I read and reflected on short passages from the New Testament. I also prayed each night to a God that I did not know very much about but whom I felt was owed some allegiance. My family was not a religious one; my father was agnostic and my mother followed what she had been taught at a religious girls' school.

My mother had a lovely soprano singing voice and was asked to lend her voice to the Upper Beaconsfield Choir services, so I did have some knowledge of the traditions of the church services. I chose to be confirmed at fourteen but was almost stripped of my membership when I played up in classes. Belonging to a church school, I maintained some interest in Christianity but mostly I was following the orthodoxy of the Anglican Church. At no point did I entertain the idea of challenging the teachings.

In Grantchester, a village close to Cambridge, I belonged to the Anglican church and took on the role of Sunday School teacher. This was because I could see the community value in having a Sunday School, but at no time did I believe that my role was to pass on the word of God. I think that my leadership position was severely challenged when the arrival of the Sunday School gang almost brought the congregation to an exasperated response as we trooped down the aisle and created distractions for those gathered to hear the learned words from Sir Desmond Lee.

It was not until I met a Uniting Church minister on our return to Australia that I began to see a broader and more down-to-earth view of religion. This minister sowed seeds of confidence in the validity of the church but he also planted questions about the belief in God which I had not previously considered; for example, 'Why do bad things happen to good people?' So powerful was his examination of religion that many times I expected that he would step down from the pulpit and turn to the congregation and say, 'That's it, I can no longer support this and I am stepping aside'.

My time of deep investigation into my belief began when the exposure of child abuse in the church surfaced. I was challenged to ask how a God who uses people as his voice and who also allows these people to prey on innocents. could possibly exist. The more I read and heard and talked with those inside the church the more torn I felt. I reached the point where I could no longer accept the notion of a just God who cared for all. It seemed a tragic fallacy.

Added to my response was the farcical behaviours concerning the role of women. When the western world was embracing so much about the importance of women and enabling them to take on leadership roles in business, the armed services and in the scientific world, it seemed ludicrous that patriarchy and outmoded beliefs continued to be promulgated and acted upon by those of a male gender in the church.

Now I see the conservative church in denial in so many ways and I see it inexorably declining and losing its relevance.

The church that will survive is one with community appeal. It will not necessarily have its foundations in deep theological thought, but rather the attraction of attending church will be through entertainment and being involved in music. The sermons will present the values of comradeship and the glue will be the music and food and family gatherings.

I turn my face away from the hypocrisy and instead search for meaning in nature that surrounds me and gain joy from watching a world that evolves and recognises the relevance and importance of all creatures and the part they play in the world. The value of love is played out in caring for each other and this precious planet on which we live.

Afterword

The unexamined life is not worth having, according to the famous Greek philosopher Socrates. Surely this can equally be said of personal religion.

How disappointing that so many are loath to take their personal religion down the discovery road to explore, think, examine and challenge. In their senior years, some still clutch tightly to what, in their early Sunday school or Youth Group years, they were taught about God, Jesus and the Bible. There are also those who are temperamentally inclined to go along with the crowd. They neither seek nor express a view contrary to the mob. Not for them a critical look at what they believe.

By contrast, this book champions the importance of questioning our inherited religious beliefs and values. Do they help us find our way through the rough tracks of human existence? Are they fit for the purpose of building good relationships? Do they close us in on ourselves or open us to new and better pathways? How strong is the evidence in support of what we believe? Are our beliefs so out of sync with modern science as to make them dubious at the very least? Do our beliefs and values enable us to construct a well-rounded, life affirming spirituality? Do they take us out of ourselves and set us on the venture of taking hold of a small corner of some big world problem and try to make a difference there.

For some, the answering of these questions has resulted in abandoning the faith they once had and moving on to the land of religious unbelief. Most who have taken this path speak of relief in letting go of what for them was an encumbrance or an unexamined habit. Although I have sometimes been attracted to this full on de-Christianising option I have not chosen it; well, not yet any way. I am a believer.

My intention in this book is to encourage seekers after truth to make the good parts of private religion better and to banish the bad parts. If your religion has become stale, search for a way to refresh it. If your religious outlook seems to you to have serious faults, find a way to repair the fault lines. If some religious doctrines are, in your view, absurd, dodgy or downright unbelievable, jettison them and seek better ones. If what you believe flies in the face of science, be open to the possibility that it may not be the science that needs correcting. If your inherited religious values are consistently requiring more of you than is possible for FHBs (Fallible Human Beings) then re-educate your conscience. If your God image regularly arouses fear and trembling in you rather than succour and encouragement, seek one that provides more solace. If your religious values undermine your selfhood and cripple your interactions with others, there is no reason to stick with such a self-enforced program of spiritual sabotage. If you have concluded that the Bible is an outdated document with little relevance to the modern world, try reading some recent biblical scholarship for an alternative view.

In the service of these faith-enriching tasks, *Doubt Boldly* promotes the desirability of listening to religious doubts and resolving them. Several underlying themes are stressed. One is that if there is a God worth believing in, this God's chief concern will be the welfare of humans and the salvation of the cosmos. Another is that no single religious faith is superior to others. That faith changes in individuals are inevitable, necessary and ongoing has also been promoted. This book has also alerted the reader to the possibility that we have all inherited or shaped for ourselves a life denying, sick minded, neurotic religion. The alternative has been advocated: the search for a healthy-minded, life enriching faith. Lastly this: faith changes are the outcome of active thinking. Mental homework gets us there. Rudyard Kipling's famous comment in support of curiosity and question asking is this: 'I have six faithful serving men (they taught me all I know). Their names are What and Why and When and How and Where and Who' Great questions in search of answer when reading or interpreting Christianity's Sacred Book.

Then there is Jesus of Nazareth. Clearly, I am pre-disposed towards Christianity, initially an accident of birth, born as I was in a predominantly Christian country and baptised as an infant. Throughout my life, however, I have found that growth transitions in this inherited religion of mine have been best achieved by keeping the focus on the once-only lived life of that enigmatic, troublesome, Palestinian-born, Jewish sage: Jesus of Nazareth.

A human he was, like the rest of us, but a whole lot more human than we are or ever could be. How much more has always been a big question in historic Christianity. Fully God and Fully Man claims various creeds, a doctrine wholly endorsed by many. In my experience however, the more he is like us humans, the more helpful he becomes as a reliable mountain guide on the pathways of human existence.

In the end we ultimately must make our own judgments about this Jesus. The cautionary note of H. G. Wells, is also worth heeding: 'The Galilean has been too much for our small hearts'.

Endnotes

1 Try for example Ryan Holiday and Stephen Hanselman, *Lives of the Stoics*, Profile Books: London 2020.
2 The explanation for this title given to Jesus is that, according to the New Testament, he grew up in Nazareth, a village in Galilee, now in northern Israel.
3 The word de-Christianisation is also be used to refer to major political-cultural shifts away from Christianity. The Reign of Terror (September 1793 to July 1794) during the French Revolution is the prominent case. The forces of secularism triumphed over Christianity; anti-clericalism took violent pathways; external symbols of Christianity such as crosses, bells and items used in worship were outlawed and destroyed; religious statues and plaques suffered the same fate; official festivals of Liberty and Reason were instituted in their place. This book does not address or discuss de-Christianisation when that is what the word refers to.
4 Leunig, *Spectrum, The Age*, 18 December 2021.
5 This material is found in *Dicey Topics, The Age*, 18 July 2020.
6 *Dicey Topics, The Age*, 29 August 2020.
7 Panentheism is described on p. xxx.
8 See Charles Birc, *Science and Soul*, UNSW Press: Sydney 2008 pp.114-117 for the quotes and material of these paragraphs
9 Of his several books that address this idea, *Science and Soul* is an excellent introduction.
10 David Lodge, *Quite a Good Time to be Born*, Penguin Random House: London 2015.
11 Ibid., p. 270.
12 Ibid., p. 410.
13 Ibid., p. 360.
14 Ibid., p. 478.
15 Kenneth Vaux, *Joseph Fletcher: Memoir of a Radical* Westminster: John Knox Press 1993
16 Ibid., p. 76.
17 Joseph Fletcher, *Situation Ethics*, SCM Press: London 1996 p. 57.
18 Ibid., p. 68.
19 Ibid., p. 152.
20 Ibid., p. 114.
21 Ibid., p. 69.
22 I have used this material and discussed it more fully in my previous book *Your Final Decision*, Morning Star Publishing: Vic 2015, pp. 75-78.

23 For various discussions on Fletcher's approach to ethics, two works are valuable. Part one of *Memoir* carries three contributions. For criticisms of his approach, see *The Situation Ethics Debate* Ed Harvey Fox Westminster; Philadelphia 1968. and Paul Ramsey *Deeds and Rules in Christian Ethics* Charles Scribner's Sons: New York 1967, pp. 145-225.
24 *Memoir*, p. 67.
25 Ibid., p. 85.
26 All the quotes on this page are found ibid., pp. 85-87.
27 Ibid., p. 86.
28 Ibid.
29 ibid p. 92.
30 Gordon Allport, *The Individual and his Religion*. Macmillan: New York 1952. p. 122.
31 AGZ study by Australian Research Council 2016 Survey.
32 Uniting Sexuality and Faith, Uniting Church Press: Melbourne 1997.
33 Hans Kung and William Jens, *A Dignified Dying*, S.C.M: London 1995, p. 115.
34 Jacqui Tafell, *The Age, Good Weekend* 18 September 2020.
35 William James, *The Variety of Religious Experience*, The Modern Library: New York 2002.
36 Ibid., p. 91.
37 Ibid., p. 151.
38 Ibid., p. 152.
39 Wayne Oates, *When Religion is Sick* Westminster Press: Philadelphia 1970. p. 20.
40 Ibid.
41 Sigmund Freud, *New Introductory Lectures on Psycho-analysis*, Carlton House: New York, p. 222.
42 Eric Fromm, *Fear of Freedom*, Routledge & Reagan Paul: London, 1960, p. 66.
43 Ibid.
44 Nikos Kazantzakis, *Report to Greco*, Simon and Schuster: New York, 1965, p. 16.
45 Bernard Ramm, *The Christian View of Science and Scripture*, Paternoster Press: London 1955 p. 203
46 *The Age*, 25 March 2021, p. 33.
47 David Wooton, *Galileo Watcher in the Skies*, Yale University: New Haven, 2010.
48 Ibid., p. 220.
49 Kirkbride Bible Co: Indiana USA, 1934, p. 186.
50 John Cornwell, *Newman's Unique Grave*, Continuum: London, 2010, p. 235

Endnotes

51 Quoted in Alistair McGrath, *The Twilight of Atheism*, Random House: London, 2004, p. 106.
52 Ibid., p. 105.
53 William Barclay, *The Letters to Philippians, Colossians, Thessalonians*, St Andrews Press: Edinburgh, 1959, p. 233.
54 John Steinbeck, Travels with Charley, Viking Press: New York, 1961, pp. 78-79.
55 John Calvin, *Institutes of the Christian Religion*, Westminster Press: Philadelphia, vol. 2, pp. 1007-1008.
56 Alistair McGrath, *The Twilight of Atheism*, Random House: London, 2004, pp. 274-75, for quotes on this section.
57 Marcus J. Borg, *Evolution of the Word*, Harper One: New York, 2012, p. 8.
58 *The Age*, Melbourne, 30 March 2023.
59 *Dictionary of the Bible*, ed. John McKenzie, Geoffrey Chapman: London, 1966, p. 825.
60 *Good Weekend, The Age*, 21 October 2022.
61 *Good Weekend, The Age*, 8 October 2021
62 LLoyd Geering, *Wrestling with God*, Bridget Books: 2006, pp. 141-174.
63 *Wrestling with God*, p. 173.
64 Ian Breward, *A History of the Churches in Australasia*, Oxford University Press: New York, 2001, p. 377.
65 Zwartz had a key role in keeping this Macnab issue in forefront of public attention with his three *Age* articles. He had had a distinguished career with the *Age*, a Diploma of Journalism, a Bachelor of Theology, and a lapsed Ph.D. in Philosophy. He is currently a senior fellow at the Centre for Public Christianity which describes itself as a subsidiary of the Bible Society of Australia and is committed to the historic teaching of the Old and New Testaments that centre on the life, death and resurrection of Jesus, as outlined in the Nicene Creed.
66 Sources for Strong's life include Charles's Strong's *Australian Church Christian Socialism*, MUP: Melbourne 2021 and Aneas MacDonald *One Hundred Years of Presbyterianism in Victoria*, Robertson & Mullens: Melbourne, 1937.
67 *One Hundred Years of Presbyterianism in Victoria*, p. 132.
68 Peter Cameron, *Heretic*, Doubleday: Sydney 1994 p. vii. This work is Cameron's narrative of events. The Presbyterian 'Church's narrative is found in Aeneas MacDonald, *One Hundred Years of Presbyterianism in Victoria*, Robertson & Mullins: Melbourne, 1937.
69 Ibid., p. 143.
70 Ibid., p. 51.
71 Phil Jarratt, *Ted Noffs*, Macmillan: Sydney, 1997, p. 42.
72 Ibid., p. 228.

73. Ibid., p. 297.
74. Ibid., p. 294.
75. Quoted in Charles Birch, *Science & Soul*, UNSW Press: Sydney, 2008, p. 131.
76. Gunther Bornkamm, *Jesus of Nazareth*, Harper and Row: London, 1960, p. 172.
77. Bertrand Russell, *Why I Am Not a Christian*, Allen & Unwin: London, 1957, p. 11.
78. *The God Delusion*, Richard Dawkins, Bantam Press: London, 2006, p. 97.
79. *Uniting in Worship*, Uniting Church Press: Melbourne, 1988, p. 78.
80. G. K. Chesterton, *Orthodoxy*, New Kensington: PA, 2013, p. 9.
81. The Reverend Dr Margaret Mayman is the Minister of St Michael's Uniting Church, Melbourne. She writes that for 25 years she has been in ministry in 'three liberal/progressive congregations' two of them in CBD locations. The website of St Michael's declares this: ' St Michael's mission to be a vibrant, inclusive, hospitable, and community - focused congregation, sharing progressive theology and practice - embracing spirituality, the arts, wellbeing, justice and compassion.'
82. *Europa Blues*, p. 34.
83. Albert Schweitzer, *My Life and Thought*, Allen & Unwin: London, 1954, p. 58.
84. An easy to read autobiography is *My Life and Thought*, Allen & Unwin: London, 1954. Charles Seaver, Albert Schweitzer *The Man and His Mind*, A&C Black: London, 1949, is a sympathetic work in two parts: one on Schweitzer's life and the other on his thought. A more recent work including a biography is James Bentley, *Albert Schweitzer: The Enigma*, Harper Collins: New York, 1992.
85. *My Life and Thought*, p. 102.
86. Albert Schweitzer, *The Quest for the Historical Jesus*, Adam and Black: London, 1910, pp. 387ff.
87. Ibid., p. 57.
88. Mark 10:17ff.
89. *My Life and Thought*, p. 56.
90. Ibid., p. 56.
91. Ibid., p. 210.
92. Schweitzer's concise quote on this is this: 'the essential element in Christianity as it was preached by Jesus and as it is comprehended in thought, is this, that it is only through Love that we can attain to communion with God. All living knowledge of God rests upon this foundation: that we experience Him in our lives as Will-to-Love.' Ibid.
93. For his discussion of this theme, cf. *Life and Thought*, pp. 162ff.
94. *The Quest*, p. 197.
95. Ibid., p. 401.

96 *Kerygma and Myth*, ed. Hans Werner Bartsh, Harper: New York, 1961, p. 3.
97 Ibid., p. 7.
98 Rudolph Bultmann & Karl Kundsin, *Form Criticism*, Harper Torchbooks: New York, 1962, p. 71.
99 Rudolph Bultmann, *Kerygma and Myth*, p. 5.
100 Ibid., p. 4.
101 Rudolph Bultmann, *Jesus Christ and Mythology*, SCM: London, 1958, p. 20.
102 Rudolph Bultmann, *Theology of the New Testament* Vol. 1, SCM: London, 1952, p. 9.
103 Ibid., p. 19.
104 *Jesus and Myth*, p. 13.
105 *Primitive Christianity*, p. 92.
106 *Theology of the New Testament*, p. 22.
107 Rudolph Bultmann and Karl Kundsin, *Form Criticism* Harper Torchbooks: New York, 1962, p. 1. Rudolph Bultmann, *Theology of the New Testament* Vol.One, SCM: London, 1959, p. 3.
108 *Jesus Christ and Mythology*, p. 40.
109 *Kerygma and Myth* p. 18.
110 Readers interested in either existentialism or Heidegger will find value in the delightful 2017 book *At The Existentialist Café* by Sarah Bakewell.
111 *Kerygma and Myth*, pp. 18-19.
112 Ibid.
113 *Form Criticism*, p. 66.
114 Alistair McGrath, *Christian Theology*, Blackwell: Oxford, 1994, p. 331.
115 *Kerygma and Myth*, pp. 37-38.
116 Ibid., p. 40.
117 All the biographical information and quotes on this page are found in Robert W. Funk *Honest to Jesus: Jesus for a New Millennium*, HarperCollins: SanFrancisco, 1996 ,pp. 3-6. For a comprehensive book on his life and achievements, read *Evaluating the Legacy of Robert W. Funk* edited by Andrew D. Scrimgeour, SBL Press: Atlanta 2018 provides a collection of papers about him and by him.
118 *Evaluating the Legacy of Robert W. Funk*, ed. Andrew D. Scrimgeour SBL Press: Atlanta 2018, p. 207. This chapter contains Funk's opening remarks at the first gathering of the Jesus Seminar in 1985.
119 *Honest to Jesus*, p.144.
120 *Honest to Jesus*, p. 41.
121 This couplet and all other italicised words in the following paragraphs are taken from Funk's *Honest to Jesus*.
122 Robert Funk, *Honest to Jesus*, HarperCollins: San Francisco 1996, p. 300.

123 Readers who are interested in the criteria for determining what was the voice of Jesus – he also called it a kind of voice print – will find help in chapters 7 & 8 of *Honest to Jesus*. He notes that since so many of the Jesus scholars had done pioneering study on the parables of Jesus, it would be possible to do further work on the speech forms of Jesus with a view to developing what looked to be authentic to him and what wasn't. Listed, studied, generalised, they formed *rules of evidence* that made it possible to distinguish what was his voice and what was that of the early church. They called this the criteria of *coherence*. A second rule of evidence was called *dissimilarity* or *distinctive*. Thus, to its surprise, the Fellows of the Seminar concluded that Jesus was not an eschatological prophet expecting the imminent end of the world because it was so out of character with his parables. In other words, this teaching was not his but that of his followers. One other rule of evidence was that words or thoughts ascribed to him when there was no one else there to hear them; his prayers in the Garden of Gethsemane, for example, were deemed not to be authentic, given that his disciples in the same account were described as asleep. These words would therefore be deemed by Funk 'to be part of the faith story of his followers'. Funk notes that a detailed account of the rules of evidence can be found in his work *The Gospel of Mark*, pp. 29-52.
124 Jon Meacham, *Thomas Jefferson*, Random House: New York, 2012, p. xxi.
125 *Evaluating the Legacy*, p. 265., Random House: New York, 2012, p. xxi.
126 Marcus J Borg, *Jesus in Contemporary Scholarship* Trinity International Press Valley Forge: Pennsylvania 1994, p.161.
127 Ibid.
128 Ibid., p. 171.
129 Ibid.
130 Ibid., p. 54.
131 Ibid., p. 98.
132 Ibid.
133 Ibid., pp. 101-116.
134 Elizabeth Schussler Fiorenza, *Toward New Heaven and a New Earth*, Orbis Books: New York, 2003, p. 7.
135 Elizabeth Schussler Fiorenza, *Empowering Memory and Movement*, p.118.
136 Ibid., p. 118.
137 Ibid., p. 123
138 Ibid., p. 23.
139 Ibid., p. 58.
140 Fiorenza, *Sharing Her Word*, T&T Clark: Edinburgh, 1998, p.112.
141 Ibid., p. 170.
142 Ibid., p. 167.
143 Ibid., p. 124.

144 Ibid., p. 115.
145 op, cit., p. 116.
146 Ibid., p. 173.
147 Ibid.
148 *Empowering Memory*, p. 489.
149 Elizabeth A. Johnson *She Who Is* Crossroad: New York 1996 p.35
150 Ibid p.120.
151 Ibid p. 87.
152 Ibid p.158.
153 Ibid p.152.
154 Ibid.
155 Ibid., p. 153.
156 Ibid., p. 151.
157 Ibid., p.153.
158 Ibid., p. 168.
159 Ibid., p. 157.
160 Ibid.
161 Ibid., p. 167.
162 Sally Douglas, *Jesus Sophia Returning to Woman Wisdom in the Bible, Practice and Prayer*, Cascade: Oregon 2023, p. xi.
163 Ibid., p. 43.
164 This case is spelled out in her *Early Church Understandings of Jesus as the Divine Female*, Bloomsbury: London 2016, pp. 1-3. This book was the publication of her doctoral research.
165 *Jesus Sophia*, p. 43.
166 Ibid., p. 115.

www.ingramcontent.com/pod-product-compliance
Lightning Source LLC
Chambersburg PA
CBHW012004090526
44590CB00026B/3872